Rough Diamonds: A Story Book

John Hollingshead

ROUGH DIAMONDS

A Story-Book.

BY JOHN HOLLINGSHEAD

(AUTHOR OF "RAGGED LONDON," "ODD JOURNEYS," "UNDER BOW BELLS
&c., &c.

ILLUSTRATED BY H. SANDERSON.

LONDON

SAMPSON LOW, SON, & CO.

47, LUDGATE HILL.

1862.

PREFACE.

THIS little bundle of Tales, in accordance with the general and growing fashion, is gathered from the pages of various Periodicals. If any of the stories have a higher object than merely to amuse the reader, it is to give a faithful picture of many common people amongst whom we must necessarily live and move. The "Rough Diamonds," who form the backbone of the Volume, are presented in such a way, though often with a farcical background, that they speak for themselves, without coarseness, in the language which they have picked out of the great well of English undefiled.

CONTENTS.

PAGE

I. The Old House 5

II. An Absurd Story 49

III. Nobody's Child 71

IV. What is a Pound ? 82

V. An Early-closing Problem . , . . 97

VI. The Phantom Genius 106

ROUGH DIAMONDS.

THE OLD HOUSE.

PART I.

SOME few years ago, there stood, not far from the river, to the east of London, an old, many-shaped, detached house, which was occupied by a middle-aged, common-place, pompous gentleman, of the name of Gudgeons. He was the secretary to some public company (I believe a great gas or water company); and a man who believed in no one—not even in the chairman and board of directors—so much as in himself. He knew everything—at least, so he thought; he was prepared for every emergency—at least, so he believed. His life was insured in the oldest and safest office; his property was insured in another office, equally old and equally safe; he dealt with the best butcher, the best grocer, and the best baker; he knew the exact position of the nearest fire-engine and the nearest fire-escape; and he knew the names and addresses of the best physicians for different kinds of disease. He was always supplied with a chest of the very best medicine from Apothecaries' Hall, and a cellar of the best wine from the leading wine-merchant. His servants were carefully selected, and an ample and precise record kept of their character-pedigree, from the earliest traces of their servitude. His plate and property were securely locked up every night in a large iron safe in his own bed-chamber; his fire-arms were always well loaded, within reach, and in a place of safety; and the entrances to his dwelling were provided with an ample supply of the best scientific alarums. What had Mr. Gudgeons to fear from accident, disease, or crime? What, indeed?

Mr. Gudgeons's family consisted of his wife, a nice quiet woman, of no very great ability, and three children—a girl-baby, aged eleven months, and two boys, aged respectively seven and eight years. In governing this family, he had his own peculiar notions upon education. History he considered to be a great mistake, especially when it went further back than forty or fifty years. No man ought to encumber his brains with anything except the times and the society in which he lived. The battle of Waterloo was the last decisive contest of the world; beyond that it was fruitless to go: and there the schoolmaster of the two Masters Gudgeons was particularly requested to stop. Besides regulating the instruction of his boys by day, he imparted additional information to them at night. Blue-books were brought home from the office, and Master Tom, the youngest, and Master Harry, the eldest, were examined, even at their early age, upon their knowledge of population, imports, exports, banking, joint-stock companies, and the statistics of crime.

"Papa," asked the eldest boy, on one occasion, during these distasteful catechisms, "who was the Duke of Monmouth?"

"Yes, papa," rejoined the youngest, emboldened by the example of his brother; "and who was Perkin Warbeck?"

The first question was bad enough, but the second was infinitely worse. Mr. Gudgeons was not prepared with any precise information concerning either of these historical personages; and the boys were therefore reproved for their idle curiosity, and sent to bed.

If Mr. Gudgeons had his prejudices concerning remote history, his dislike for fiction amounted to positive horror. "Novels sir," he was fond of saying over his dinner-table—"pooh! rubbish! trash! Who writes them? Chairmen of public companies don't? Directors of public companies don't? Secretaries of public companies don't."

It was impossible, however, to keep Master Tom and Master Harry from the bane of knowing "Robinson Crusoe" and "Sinbad the Sailor;" and as the books containing the stories of these interesting individuals were carefully excluded from the house, the two boys were driven to gratify their natural appetite for the wonderful upon much more questionable food.

Mr. Gudgeons was one evening unexpectedly passing the door of the room set aside as a nursery, when he heard a voice reading aloud, which he recognised as belonging to the nursemaid, Sarah Finch. Curiosity prompted Mr. Gudgeons to listen, and further, to look through a crevice in the door, when he discovered his two sons seated open-mouthed by the side of the servant, engrossed by the interest of the narrative she was reading.

"'Never,' ejaculated the Count in a voice of thunder," said Sarah Finch, reading from the book; "'never!' and raising his dagger, he was about to plunge it into the bosom of the unfortunate Countess, when the old hag of the forest seemed to dart through the wall, and before the guilty Count could recover himself, he was lying on the floor, while the Countess and the old woman had disappeared together."

Mr. Gudgeons retired at once to his best drawing-room, where Mrs. Gudgeons was seated, and rang the bell for Sarah Finch and the two boys. In a few moments they came, but not without a foreboding as to the cause of their summons.

"Well!" said Mr. Gudgeons to Sarah Finch, with all his dignity and authority thrown into an attempt at sarcasm, "so the Count cried 'Never,' in a voice of thunder, did he? He raised his dagger to plunge it into the Countess, when the old hag of the forest appeared through the floor, did she?"

"I beg your pardon, sir," said Sarah Finch, "I was only reading to amuse the young gentlemen."

"And do you suppose," continued Mr. Gudgeons, "that the young gentlemen—that my sons—can be amused with such a string of absurdities as that? Do I ever ejaculate 'Never,' in a voice of thunder? Do I ever raise a dagger to plunge it into your mistress? and does any old hag of any old forest ever come through any floor or wall? Absurd rubbish! Where's the book?"

The book was sent for, and found to be an old novel called "The Lonely One of the Heath," printed very badly upon very yellow sugar-paper, much worn and plastered with dirt at the edges, and bound in two thick slices of dirty shoe-leather.

"Now, Sarah Finch," said Mr. Gudgeons, with much solemnity, taking the book, "I shall destroy this idiotic volume of trash; and if I find you again indulging in such books, or bringing them under the notice of my children, I shall be compelled to discharge you upon the spot, with a very indifferent character. You can go. Thomas and Henry, retire to bed."

Sarah Finch returned to the nursery, vexed at the loss of her book, and the two boys went to bed.

The nursery of Mr. Gudgeons's house was a room on a level with the drawing-rooms, but apart from the rest of the building. Below it was another apartment, used as a store and lumber department, and both the rooms evidently belonged to a house of much older date than the mansion to which they appeared to be rather inharmoniously attached. The store-room was so loaded with old furniture, and disfigured with modern shelves, which had been erected to contain the preserves and other articles, that little remained of its original aspect to strike the eye, except a tone much more gloomy than the rest of the house. The nursery having been very little altered, or re-decorated, retained its original features—a dark oaken wainscoting; a lofty, murky ceiling, and plastered-over rafters; a fire-place, in which a tall man could stand upright, with much carving in oak all round the sides and along the mantle-shelf, almost black with smoke and age; dark, polished, oaken flooring boards, very narrow, smooth, and closely bound together; and a large arched window in a recess, looking out on the garden. There was an old beech-tree about ten yards from this window, in the garden, whose broad, thick trunk added to the sombre appearance of this room and the store-room below. The mossy branches of this tree spread outwards in all directions, some passing over the roof of the main mansion, others over the roof of this ancient outbuilding. The nursery was very scantily furnished, for it was the play-room of the children by day, as it was the bedchamber of Sarah Finch, the nurse, by night. Her bed stood in an arched cupboard recess, on the right as you entered the door, which was near the wall on the garden side. At the other corner, still on the right of the entrance door, and against the main mansion, was another arched recess, which contained nothing but two cotton dresses belonging to Sarah Finch. This recess had doors, which closed it in, but the doors of the recess where the bed stood had been taken away, their place being supplied with curtains.

Sarah Finch was an ordinary young woman, about thirty, inclined to be fat, considered trustworthy and steady, not attached to any follower, properly vaccinated, with no tendency to lunacy

or scrofula, fond of children, born near Cambridge, father dead,
mother living; had been in two other situations, where she had
lived respectably and respectively six years and three years;
and she had already been in Mr. Gudgeons's family near four
years. These were the particulars contained in Mr. Gudgeons's
book of servants' characters, each fact being duly entered in
a separate column, and the whole signed " Sarah Finch," in a
handwriting not unlike that of poor Guido Fawkes when he
was taken from the rack.

Sarah Finch's hour of retiring to rest was half-past ten, when
Mrs. Gudgeons came to see if the candle was properly extinguished; and at half-past ten she retired as usual on this
particular night. Her duties had been slightly increased during
the last fortnight by the task of weaning young Miss Elizabeth,
or Bessy Gudgeons, as she was called, aged eleven months.
This broke Sarah Finch's rest, which she did not much like,
but it gave her some kind of companion by way of reward. Of
course she had complained to her master (her mistress had
little voice in the management of the house) about the large,
gloomy character of her sleeping apartment; and, of course, her
complaints had been treated with the contempt they deserved.
Her request to have the cook, or the waiting-maid, sent down
to sleep with her was not complied with, because the recess was
only large enough to contain a bed for one, and the whole
apartment was required during the day as a play-room for the
boys. Any nervous timidity she may have exhibited, was very
quickly put down by a gentleman of such a practical and
unimaginative turn of mind as Mr. Gudgeons.

Miss Bessy Gudgeons, considering her age, bore her weaning
process very amiably. She slept in a small iron cot, which was
squeezed into the recess by the side of Sarah Finch's bed, and,
after being fed with a bottle before retiring to rest (about seven
o'clock in the evening), nothing more was heard of her by her

nurse until about two o'clock in the morning. when she required
to be fed again. Sarah Finch was a sound sleeper, and a good
sharp cry was necessary to wake her.

It was daylight the next morning when Sarah Finch aw ke
—daylight on a November morning. about seven o'clock.
Rubbing her eyes, she looked into the little iron bedstead for
the child, and not seeing it very clearly, she rubbed them again,
to discover that it was not there. She put her hand under her
own pillow in an instant, and found the bottle of food, wrapped
up in flannel to keep it warm: it was untouched. Leaping
from the bed, she looked underneath it, round the recess, over
the room, in the other recess, and finally she ran to the door to
find it still locked, as she had locked it last night after Mrs.
Gudgeons had left.

Sarah Finch was not strong-minded, nor particularly super-
stitious; and under the painful and mysterious circumstances
in which she was placed, she behaved with very praiseworthy
coolness. She hurriedly put on some clothing, and proceeded
nervously and anxiously to the sleeping apartment of Mr. and
Mrs. Gudgeons. She knocked sharply at the door, and was
answered by Mr. Gudgeons, who was a tolerably early riser,
and who appeared with his face half covered with shaving
lather.

"Now, then," said Mr. Gudgeons, "what's the matter?"

"Is the baby here, sir?" asked Sarah Finch, breathlessly.

"Certainly not!" returned Mr. and Mrs. Gudgeons, simul-
taneously.

"Then it's gone, sir, as sure as I stand here!" said the distressed nurse; "stolen out of the room at night, mum! Oh, I
told you so, sir! I never liked the room; I knew they would.
Oh, good gracious!" Here Sarah Finch took the liberty of
fainting before her master, just as he and Mrs. Gudgeons were
about to overwhelm her with a variety of anxious questions.

The household was soon alarmed, and, leaving Sarah Finch in the care of the waiting-maid, Mr. Gudgeons went at once to the nursery, where his wife had gone before him.

" Am I asked to believe," said Mr. Gudgeons, after examining the fastenings of the windows, and looking round the room, "that thieves break into my house without disturbing my alarums, and only steal a baby ?"

" Babies can't go without hands," said Mrs. Gudgeons, sobbing. " If I could only see the poor little dear in its little coffin, I should know it was happy."

" Yes, mum," said the cook, who had come into the room, "just as it took so much notice too, mum. Don't take on so, mum, I beg."

Mr. Gudgeons was a man of decision, and did not waste much time in idle grief. " James," he said to the gardener and general man-servant, who had joined the cook, " I leave Sarah Finch in your custody. Jane," this was to the cook, " fetch a cab."

The cab was fetched, and Mr. Gudgeons got into it. He believed in excellence only when it was well advertised. If his wife's leg had been broken, he would have driven to Sir Lambert Daniel, the celebrated surgeon ; if it had been a case of family cholera, he would have driven to Doctor Calomel, the great physician ; if a serious accident had happened to his horse, he would have driven to Mr. Spavin, the renowned veterinary practitioner : and, as his baby had been stolen, he drove to the well-known Secret Investigation Office of Messrs. Meadows and Winks.

PART II.

IT was rather an early hour to go to any office upon business; but the profession of Messrs. Meadows and Winks was a peculiar profession, and there was a principal in attendance at every hour of the day and night.

When a man goes to a firm of two or more members, for the first time, he generally asks for the partner whose name may head the list, and without knowing what that person's measure of ability may be, or even if there is really such an individual in existence, he feels excessively disappointed when informed he is not within, and is not expected in town for several weeks. This was particularly the case with Mr. Gudgeons, who always liked to have everything of the best, or what was duly advertised as such. When told by a stout, florid man in heavy boots, and a large shooting-coat, that Mr. Meadows had only just started for Copenhagen, Australia, New Orleans, and a few such places, after a runaway clerk from Liverpool, Mr. Gudgeons's vexation vented itself in loud expressions of dissatisfaction.

" It's not enough," he said, " that I, who never had my pocket picked, am suddenly to become the victim of the most absurd robbery that ever happened to a respectable member of society ; but the very best man in London to discover the crime, has just gone to the North Pole after an ordinary runaway felon !"

" Well, sir," said Mr. Winks, for that member of the detective firm it was who had answered Mr. Gudgeons, " you needn't put yourself about so. I daresay there's nothing about the case but what I can tackle."

" Your name, sir, is——? " inquired Mr. Gudgeons.

" Winks, of Meadows and Winks," returned the junior partner, stopping further questions.

" Very well," said Mr. Gudgeons, " step into this cab, and come along with me."

Mr. Winks put on his hat, took up a thick stick, and then went to a speaking-tube in the corner of the room.

" If that murder, or that forgery comes in this morning," said Mr. Winks, up the pipe, " I'm gone with a gent. for a few hours. Now, sir," turning to Mr. Gudgeons, " I'm at your service."

This looked business-like and unromantic, and so far Mr. Gudgeons was satisfied; but he was not favourably disposed to junior partners, though his peculiar position compelled him to accept Mr. Winks's assistance. He stated the case to that gentleman in the cab, and in about half-an-hour they were standing in the nursery of Mr. Gudgeons's family mansion. Everything was much the same as Mr. Gudgeons had left it, except that the women, especially Mrs. Gudgeons, appeared with very red eyes, and were rather favourably disposed to a supernatural explanation of the mystery. The two boys had perfectly agreed between themselves as to the present condition and prospects of their lost sister. They never for a moment suspected Sarah Finch. They had had their doubts about one Robinson Crusoe, until they considered how he was shut up on an inaccessible island; they had even suspected Sinbad the Sailor, until they recollected he had got quite enough trouble on his own hands without encumbering himself with a stolen baby; and at last they settled upon the old hag of the forest, who was remarkably fond of children, having none of her own. Their youthful imaginations pictured the lost little one lying in a golden cavern, upon a bed of scented leaves, feeding upon large peaches, without a fear of indigestion, listening to the most wonderful musical-box ever heard in this world; and, above all, far away from odious lessons upon population, and the statistics of crime.

This was the very natural result of the mysterious robbery, which annoyed Mr. Gudgeons the most. He had the proper feelings of a father—at least it is to be presumed so, as his children wanted for nothing which money could purchase; but he also had his theories and opinions to preserve. He hated the romantic—he did not believe in the wonderful; and just as he had begun to flatter himself upon having thoroughly grounded his boys in his own way of thinking, the whole fabric of his pet education was swept away by an occurrence which defied the ordinary rules of explanation.

Mr. Winks did not appear to be a person of any very great powers of mind; in fact, his greatest successes (and he had had them, as well as Mr. Meadows) were effected by remaining perfectly passive; and his reputation (and he had got one, as well as Mr. Meadows) was acquired by opening his ears and holding his tongue. He was the representative of a system, very simple in its operation, though sometimes very useful in its results. He waited until somebody came to his office with something to say, and in general he had not to wait very long. The information he bought he sold again at a premium; and there was little in the working of his trade more wonderful than this.

The unusual character of the robbery he had been called in to investigate rather puzzled Mr. Winks, though he was too discreet to betray himself. In conversation he openly treated the supposed mystery as a thing of every-day occurrence; though, privately, he could not refer it to any class of crime with which his professional experience had made him familiar. He looked round the room, and found no signs of violence, no traces of burglars, or burglary. The window (well provided with Mr. Gudgeons's favourite alarums) had not been touched; the lock of the door had not been tampered with; there were no signs throughout the house of forcible entrance; and although there was little in the room of any value, nothing had disappeared, except the baby. Baby-stealing, when carried on by women—chiefly beggars—in the streets, fell naturally into its appointed place, and did not disturb the harmony of the great criminal system; but, in its present form, it was a sudden and meteoric appearance; and Mr. Winks, for the present, got out of the difficulty he was in by a very obvious and a very common-place mode of investigation.

" I should like to see the nurse," said Mr. Winks.

" Certainly," said Mr. Gudgeons, and he ordered Sarah Finch.

Sarah made her appearance, looking very wild and nervous; both bad symptoms in the mind of Mr. Winks.

" Have you any followers, Sarah Finch?" asked Mr. Winks.

" None, sir," replied the distressed nurse.

" Never had any?" still inquired Mr. Winks.

" Never, sir," still answered the nurse.

" Don't know anything of a sailor, named Tarboy?"

" No, sir."

" Don't know anything of a discharged postman, named John Knox?"

" No; of course not."

" Don't know anything of a ticket-of-leave man, No. 4,236—dressed in a grenadier's uniform?"

" Certainly not," replied Sarah Finch, becoming gradually more spirited as she was losing her temper. These men were pure fabrications of the inventive Mr. Winks, but in putting such questions he was impressing Mr. Gudgeons with a sense of his stores of information, and acting upon the time-honoured traditions of his art.

" Where were you born?" asked Mr. Winks, continuing his examination.

" Not a hundred miles from Cambridge," returned the badgered nurse, now fully aroused, and partially sulky.

" Are your parents still living?"

" Mr. Winks," said Mr. Gudgeons, at this point, feeling that the course the examination was taking reflected upon his own management of his household, " I'm happy to say my establish-

ment is not conducted without some order and method; and
I have a full record of answers to all these questions you are
now putting to that wretched woman."

This last expression of her master was extremely distasteful
to the excited Sarah Finch.

" Wretched woman, sir, you may well say," she said, " to
have to live in a house, and sleep in a room like this. You
don't suppose I've eaten the poor dear baby, do you? Give
me my long character, and let me go."

" Sarah Finch," returned Mr. Gudgeons, with much dignity
and solemnity, " leave the room. You will consider yourself
in custody until this affair is explained."

Sarah did as she was ordered, sobbing aloud, for her bursts
of spirit were very fitful, and they soon burned out.

Mr. Winks looked very solemn, stroked his chin, and shook
his head, all of which might mean nothing at all, or might mean
a great deal.

" Now, sir," said Mr. Gudgeons, rather loudly, getting impatient, for with all his weakness he was not a man to be trifled
with; " what next?"

Mr. Winks saw the necessity of earning his money, and he
pushed on.

" There's a tree outside that window," said Mr. Winks.

" Good," returned Mr. Gudgeons, concisely.

" Its distance from the wall is—what?"

" Ten yards," replied Mr. Gudgeons.

" It passes over the roof of this outbuilding?" continued
Mr. Winks, who had made a survey.

" It does," replied Mr. Gudgeons, " and the nearest branch
that would bear a man's weight, or even a boy's, is about
fifteen yards in a slightly slanting direction from the roof."

" Exactly," said Mr. Winks; " the garden wall, which divides
you from the road and a field, is lofty and well protected with
broken glass; there are no footsteps traceable in the garden;

but still, a rope slung round the nearest branch of that tree would furnish access to the roof; and that once gained, there is an easy road to the room down the broad old chimney."

"Good," returned Mr. Gudgeons.

"That is the only possible road," continued Mr. Winks, "by which a professional burglar could enter; but, as a man of the world, you must know that professional burglars don't risk their lives and liberty to steal a baby."

"Exactly my opinion," replied Mr. Gudgeons.

"Very well, then," returned Mr. Winks; "suspicion points strongly to the members of your own household, especially to Sarah Finch."

"Where's her motive for such conduct?" said Mr. Gudgeons.

"Have you had any words with her lately?" asked Mr. Winks.

"A few, last night," replied Mr. Gudgeons, "about a trashy book she was reading to my two boys."

"Not sufficient for the act, but there's no accounting for many of these things. Do you feel disposed to give her into formal custody?"

"No," returned Mr. Gudgeons, promptly; "I certainly do not. My object in applying to you was to avoid publicity. My servants are forbidden to speak of this affair abroad. The child's lost, and it must be found; but I don't want to be advertised as the football with whom every thief or madman is at liberty to play. I don't want my house made a nine-days' wonder—there's nothing wonderful in it—nor a hundred people calling upon me under pretence of condolement, but, in reality, only to satisfy their curiosity."

"There's only one course, then, left open," said Mr. Winks.

"What's that?" asked Mr. Gudgeons.

"I must advertise, in my own way, and wait."

PART III.

THE most dreary, dismal spots upon earth, either in summer or in winter, but especially on a gloomy, drizzling November day, are those bits of hopelessly waste ground in a thoroughly low neighbourhood, in the heart or the outskirts of the metropolis. Whether they are open and unprotected, or walled in with a few boards, and even placarded as " to let," they are all so marvellously alike, considering the materials of which they are composed, that the faithful picture of one may stand as the model of them all. They are the resting-places of rubbish; the cemeteries of things which still retain some shadowy spirit of humanity, although they are now worthless, even to the rag-picker or the tramp. There is always that wretched, mouldy upper-leather of a shoe, whose sole has parted from it for ever in the weary pilgrimage of life; there are always those old, weird, rotten, battered saucepans, that look like hats—and those equally miserable, discarded, tattered hats, that look like the old saucepans; there is always that piece of an old straw bonnet, surrounded by a number of large thick oyster-shells, pieces of white gleaming china, and pieces of blue willow-pattern plates; there are always a few dust-heaps, fragments of ginger-beer bottles and broken glass, lumps of rain-rotted placards, a little rank grass, the sole of a child's boot, and a dead dog and cat. The effect is dismal: for we see nothing amongst the worn-out, useless, discarded fragments, but what has, at one time, been the faithful servant, or the chosen companion, of man.

Along the border of a waste of this kind, not far from the river, and in a crowded part of the metropolis, called Deadman's Fields, was a line of low houses—almost huts—inhabited by a population of a half-savage, dangerous nature. Their existence was a disgrace; their source of living was rather guessed at than known; their bodies were strong, though the food they

ate was coarse, the water they drank was foul, and the air they
breathed was worse than impure; they were ignorant in book-
knowledge, had never heard of Lord Brougham and the "Penny
Magazine," but their intellects were keen, and they made their
influence felt. Social reformers talked a good deal about them
—and that was all. At a time of general disease, a bricklayer-
missionary was sent by a public board with a pail of whitewash
to purify their homes; and his ear sometimes detected the clink
of gold, in places where the children seemed to be hungering
for bread.

There was no equality—even here. Some were ambitious,
flew high, fell, or became distinguished amongst their fellows.
Others plodded on in mean, obscure paths, all chosen for the
same reason—living without work; all leading to the same
end—the jail.

In one of these houses or huts, at this time, there lived a
man named Dick Muzzle, who was no better than his neighbours, and no worse. His original name was Dick Turpin
Muzzle, given him by his parents in admiration of the immortal
highwayman; but, as Dick did not come up to the expectations
of his family and friends, the "Turpin" got by degrees
obliterated from his name, and he was simply known, at last,
as Dick Muzzle.

Dick, being of weak heart, though of strong body, had for a
long time occupied a position equally suspended between the
criminal and the sporting world. Sometimes he trained dogs,
for fighting and other amusing purposes; at others, he stole
dogs for sale and other profitable purposes. By degrees, however, the sporting world altered, and proved unkind. Dick's
fashionable patrons (and he once had many, who went from
the dog-pit to the boudoir or drawing-room) dropped off, one
by one, perhaps under an improved tone of public humanity,
perhaps in search of another hobby; and Dick, at last, was
thrown for subsistence upon an undivided profession. If any

compiler of a London Directory had asked Dick's calling now, he would have been answered, " dog-fancier," which means, a person who fancies every dog of any value that ever comes in his way.

Dick Muzzle, notwithstanding his great social abasement, had found a woman willing to become his lawful wedded wife; and the fruit of this marriage was two boys, who were now respectively about seven and eight years of age.

The home of these children had always been the streets and the piece of waste land before their father's house. They were thin and ill-clad; they were dirty and untaught; but they were active as deer; their eyes were sharp and bright as rats' eyes; they had strong wills for such children, nerve, courage, and keen watchfulness, and knowledge of the world—such a world as they saw every day of their lives. Night or day, they went where they liked, did what they liked; no one questioned them, no one restrained them. Sometimes they tumbled by the sides of omnibuses, rolling round like wheels, coming on their bare feet with a loud smack, and scanning the faces of the outside passengers in an instant from end to end, with the actions of monkeys and the eyes of weasels. Sometimes they held horses; sometimes they raked in the river mud at low water for what they could find; sometimes they fought like terriers for money thrown to them by passengers over one of the bridges. They were known in the neighbourhood as Old Mudlark and Young Mudlark, although there was very little difference between them, either in size, activity, or intelligence.

They had occasionally assisted their father in his business, but not to any extent, as they possessed too much life to settle down so early in the tame pursuit of dog-stealing. They knew the breed, nature, and value of dogs, and they knew what a good dog meant in the home of their childhood. It meant meat, potatoes, beer, gin, and generally a comfortable state of things; no dog meant no meat, no potatoes, no beer, no gin, and generally a very uncomfortable state of things. Therefore they saw the importance of dogs; and this was logic, though they had not learned it in the schools.

For some few days past, it had been no dog in Dick Muzzle's establishment, and things were looking rather gloomy. There were two old bull-terriers upstairs, but they were kept as decoys, and they were wholly unsaleable, if their master had even attempted to part with them. There was no other property available for realisation in Dick's house, as a glance round the place would have shown to any observer. There were only two rooms—one above, one below. The street-door opened into the sitting-room, disclosing an old turn-up bedstead, four Windsor chairs, a deal table, a ragged mat, a few other necessary articles of no value, and a smoky picture of the cock-pit at Westminster. The upper room was reached through a trap-door in the corner, by a pair of moveable steps, and when reached it only showed a very dirty, wretched sleeping apartment. There were several dogs'-houses, and the two bull-terriers in this room; and the trap-door closed down, so that you could stand upon it with perfect safety.

Dick Muzzle came down stairs about nine o'clock in the morning of the sixth day on which there had been no dog, and sat moodily smoking his pipe over an empty grate, with both his feet on the fender, and his elbows upon his knees. He did not notice that both the brothers Mudlark were out; and if he had, he would not have known whether they had been away all night, or had started early in the morning. The general habits of the house were not those of a well-regulated family.

Dick Muzzle had been sitting smoking and ruminating in this position perhaps about half an hour, when the head of his youngest born—Young Mudlark—was thrust in watchfully at the door, and withdrawn again, in an instant, with animal rapidity. There was meaning in this, as was soon shown; for in another few minutes the same young outcast bounded into the room with bare feet, and the agility of an acrobat.

" Come hout, yer warmin'," said Dick Muzzle, who was not in a humour to be trifled with. Young Mudlark made no reply, except by turning a Catherine-wheel hand-spring across the room, and before the father could make up his mind what this conduct deserved, the eldest of the two young Mudlarks made his appearance at the door, with a bundle done up in a small thick blanket.

" Halloo ! " said the father, " what game d'ye call this ? "

" A babby," replied the eldest Mudlark, with some pride, while the youngest performed the most extravagant antics in his unbounded delight.

" A what ? " said the father, putting down his pipe, and opening his eyes in astonishment.

" A babby," repeated the eldest born, nursing up his burthen. Mrs. Muzzle had by this time come down the steps from the bed-room loft, and had joined the family group.

" Where'd you get it ? " she asked, taking the bundle from her son.

" Found it, o' coorse," said both the Mudlarks, in chorus.

" Where'd you get it ? " repeated the father, loudly.

" Prigg'd it from a p'ram'later, then," returned the elder, sulkily.

" How d'ye mean ? " said the father, not understanding the term.

" From a young-un's shay, then," replied the eldest Mudlark, in explanation.

" Oh ! " said Dick Muzzle, drawing a breath of relief.

There was a short pause in the conversation at this point, during which Mrs. Muzzle, who was a mother herself, opened the blanket, and found a genteel, healthy, sleeping female child, about a twelvemonth old.

" What am I to do wi' a babby ? " asked Dick Muzzle,

vacantly, his intellect not being very quick to perceive the profit of any new source of crime that was brought before him.

" You know, fast enough," said the eldest Mudlark, sharply; " a babby's better nor a dog, ain't it ? A gent gives five pund for 'is dog; a coorse he'll guv more for his babby, won't he ? "

This business-like statement altered Dick Muzzle's manner at once, and he could not conceal his admiration for the talent of his first-born.

" Eh ? " he said, turning to Mrs. Muzzle, with a gratified twinkle in his eye, and pointing with his thumb over his shoulder to the eldest Mudlark, " he ain't a bad sort, is he ? He knows a thing or two ! "

The infant that had found its way, thus far without injury, into the bosom of the Muzzle family, was the lost baby—Miss Elizabeth, or Bessy Gudgeons. The story about the perambulator was of course false; but as neither Mr. nor Mrs. Muzzle seemed to doubt it, the two outcast boys preserved their secret. In whatever way they had got at the child, their motive for stealing it was clearly conveyed in their own words. The home of their childhood was suffering under adversity for want of a good dog. A good dog they had not found, but they had discovered a respectable baby, and a respectable baby, they reasoned, must be equal to several good dogs. This, again, was logic, though they had not learned it in the schools.

There is some little pride lingering in the hearts of even the very lowest specimens of humanity; and Mrs. Muzzle's boast was that she herself was a mother. Social reformers, looking at her two boys, might, perhaps, have thought it would have been better for society, if she had not been quite so productive. The maternal instinct, however, in this case, had its beneficial use, for it procured a large degree of careful attention for little Bessy Gudgeons. When the child woke up, it was very hungry, and it ate some coarse bread and water, made into a rude pap, with a relish that would have astonished Sarah

Finch; and the finishing touch was put to the process of its weaning, in a way that poor Mrs. Gudgeons had never dreamed of. A comfortable bed was made for the child (chiefly of straw) in a large dog's-house upstairs, which had once been the habitation, and was now sacred to the memory, of " Black-nosed Billy," the most celebrated fighting-dog of his day. Mrs. Muzzle considered it a perfect palace of a cradle —there is no accounting for taste. The two old bull-terriers whined and whistled with satisfaction when they saw the preparations being made for a new companion ; and little Bessy Gudgeons seemed to be very well satisfied with her quarters, and also with her new nurse.

While Mrs. Muzzle was busy, Dick Muzzle was not idle ; and the first thing he did was to send the youngest Mudlark for the " doctor." This did not mean that any one was ill, but only that the services of a particular man in that particular criminal community were required. Criminals are like a good many other classes of society : they have talent, but they want capital. Their gains are precarious, and they have a tendency to outlive their means, in which position they pledge the proceeds of the next robbery before they are actually realised.

The doctor for whom Dick Muzzle had sent, was a capitalist in the confined sense of the term, and a man who could read, and write, and cipher. His acquirements were in active demand in every negociation requiring any share of literary knowledge ; and his money was quite as much in demand, for small loans, based upon securities of a not very marketable nature.

The doctor's transactions with Dick Muzzle were very simple. When a good dog was found, the doctor was called in to advance a small sum in proportion to the value of the animal. This he invariably did at a high rate of interest, reserving to himself the right of superintending its restitution to its rightful owner, and of receiving the reward, and paying himself very

handsomely out of the money for his pains. The modern
system of usury could not have been better understood by the
doctor, if he had been a lawyer and a money-lender, practising
in the most refined circles.

The doctor was called in to look at the baby, and the two
young Mudlarks were sharply on the watch, for they believed
in the doctor much more than they did in their own father.
They saw him always well dressed, always handling money,
never in trouble, never taken into custody, like some of their
neighbours; and the boys never lost an opportunity of listening
to what he said, in the hope of discovering the secret of his
prosperity. The doctor had assisted at too many varieties of
crime to be astonished at being asked to lend money upon a
stolen baby. He examined the child with an experienced eye,
and soon satisfied himself of its grade and quality. The few
questions he put to the two boys (who consistently maintained
their story about the perambulator) confirmed his impression.
He spoke confidentially to Dick Muzzle at the door, and the
quick eye of the eldest Mudlark detected the glitter of several
sovereigns passing from the doctor's hand to his father's.
The quick ear of the eldest Mudlark also heard the doctor say
something about " properly managing the child, so as to produce a hundred pounds;" and it made a deep impression upon
his youthful and imaginative mind.

The bargain was sealed, and the infant daughter of Mr.
Gudgeons—Mr. Gudgeons, who had money in the funds, a
good banker's balance, and unencumbered landed property
besides—was mortgaged in a low hovel by an operation between
two individuals, one being a professional dog-stealer, and the
other being the dog-stealer's patron, adviser, and friend.

PART IV.

WHEN Mr. Winks returned to his office, he at once caused it to be intimated, through the channels at his command, that he was prepared to purchase a baby. He also drew up an advertisement, couched in vague and mysterious terms, and inserted in curious, out-of-the-way publications, wherein he stated, that, for a female child, with two teeth and a fair complexion, whose age did not exceed eleven months or one year, he could give a certain number of sterling pounds.

Mr. Winks was an old-established family man, but still he wanted another baby!

Many applications were made to Mr. Winks in the course of the next day, which he waited at home to receive, and at last he became possessed of the right communication. A respectable man called upon him, all alone, saw him all alone, and said he thought he could provide him with a baby exactly like the one he required. An appointment was made for the following afternoon: the time, four o'clock; the place, "the good dry skittle-ground" of the "Beau Brummell" public-house, Mire Street, Deadman's Fields.

Mr. Winks immediately acquainted Mr. Gudgeons with this arrangement, according to orders; for the latter gentleman still had his doubts about trusting entirely to a junior partner, and he insisted upon taking an active part at every important step in this very troublesome and peculiar business. Mr. Winks would have preferred conducting this negociation himself, but Mr. Gudgeons, as usual, had determined to have his own way, and Mr. Winks was compelled to humour him.

At four o'clock in the afternoon of the next day (the second from the one on which the child had disappeared), Mr. Gudgeons, well-supplied with metallic currency for a ready-money transaction, proceeded, in company with Mr. Winks, to buy back his lost child from the hands of the dangerous classes

It was a pity that Mr. Gudgeons had thrust himself forward
in this matter, for he was, of all men, the least adapted to treat
it with the unprejudiced coolness it required. He could not be
made to understand why he was to appear as the purchaser of
an infant, and not as a fierce, foaming, injured father, loudly
demanding the restitution of his stolen child.

"A gang of ruffians—a pack of scoundrels!" he shouted in
the cab, as they reached their place of destination. "There,
sir! I tell you what I'd do if I was a magistrate: I'd transport
every man who dared to live in such a blackguard neighbourhood!"

"My dear sir," said Mr. Winks, calmly, "you must really
command your temper, or you will spoil all."

They got out of the cab at the "Beau Brummell," a low,
dingy public-house, not far from Dick Muzzle's dwelling, and
they were received by a respectable-looking man, who seemed
prepared for their arrival. This was the "doctor," and the
same person who had called upon Mr. Winks on the day before.

The place was repulsive in appearance, with an ill-stocked
bar, and a strong smell of beer and sawdust; but still Mr.
Gudgeons felt no fear, and insisted, much against Mr. Winks's
wish, upon going *himself* through the interview with the man or
men in the skittle-ground. This expressed determination a
little altered the plans of the doctor. If Mr. Winks had conducted the negociation in person for the return of the stolen
baby, the doctor would have appeared as the representative of
Dick Muzzle; but as Mr. Gudgeons was about to take Mr.
Winks's position, Mr. Winks would require looking after during
the interview by a competent person; and this very necessary
task the doctor undertook to perform, while Dick Muzzle met
the decisive Mr. Gudgeons.

The skittle-ground was of course at the back of the house,
and approached by two back-ways, or alleys, which came up to
its single door almost at a right angle with each other. At the

entrance to both these courts a man was standing, as if by accident, while the doctor took up his post with Mr. Winks, guarding the approach from the house. When Mr. Gudgeons entered the skittle-ground—a kind of place he had never been in before in his life—Dick Muzzle affected to be earnestly employed in solving some intricate problem with two pins, a ball, and two pieces of dead-wood.

"Now, then," said Mr. Gudgeons, very testily; "my time's valuable."

"Oh!" said Dick Muzzle, looking up from the ground, though he had before examined Mr. Gudgeons; "you're the gent as wants to buy a babby!"

"Go on," replied Mr. Gudgeons, commanding his temper with much difficulty.

"What might be yer notions, now, about the price of a hinfant?" inquired Dick Muzzle, looking artfully at Mr. Gudgeons.

If Mr. Gudgeons had consulted his own taste, he would have said, "A horsewhip;" but he restrained himself, by a great effort, in obedience to Mr. Winks's instructions, and replied, "Ten pounds."

"Ten pund!" said Dick Muzzle, with a smile of contempt, "why, I'd gi' more for a dog—a mongrel! If I'd got a nice female hinfant, wi' light 'air an' blue eyes, about a year old—mind, I never sed I 'ad—I should want a tidy sight more for it nor ten pund—ah, nor yet fifty!"

"You rascal!" exclaimed Mr. Gudgeons, now fully enraged, and advancing with a threatening air towards Dick Muzzle, "do you dare to trifle with my feelings as a father?"

"Come," returned Dick Muzzle, putting himself in a defensive attitude; "it's no huse your quarrellin' wi' me, 'cos two can play at that game. I don't know anythin' habout fathers, nor yet mothers. You come to me to buy a hinfant—werry well; p'r'aps I've got one to sell—p'r'aps I ain't."

This oration was stopped by the appearance of Mrs. Muzzle, who beckoned her husband to the door of the skittle-ground.

"It's gone!" she said, in a quick, nervous whispering tone.

"What's gone?" asked Dick Muzzle, who required full particulars of everything.

"The baby—the child," replied Mrs. Muzzle; "the two boys must 'av' run away wi' it agen, while my back was turned."

"Come," said Mr. Gudgeons, interrupting this conversation, "I can't be trifled with in this manner. Give me the child, and name your price."

"I ain't got no child," returned Dick Muzzle, rather bewildered by what his wife had told him, "I never sed I 'ad."

This was too much for Mr. Gudgeons, and he immediately sought the advice of Mr. Winks outside. It was getting dusk, and it was necessary to act at once. Mr. Winks never expected that Mr. Gudgeons, without assistance, would bring the negociation to a successful close; but, when Dick Muzzle persisted in declaring that he had no baby to sell, and never said he had, and the doctor (who had been informed of the disappearance of the child), when appealed to, merely shook his head, even Mr. Winks was fairly puzzled, though he did not think proper to admit it. Mr. Gudgeons threw no additional light upon the mystery, by relating the appearance of the woman, Mrs. Muzzle (who came and went along one of the back alleys); and Mr. Winks decided that there was nothing in this sudden change of tactics, but a desire to extort a higher price for the child.

"You know me," said Mr. Winks to the doctor and Dick Muzzle, "and you know my office. My friend is determined to buy a baby, and he won't give more for it than fifty pounds. It's now five o'clock, and we shall both return to my office, where we shall wait until ten o'clock. If no one fetches us to buy a baby for fifty pounds by that hour, we shall have to go elsewhere—you understand."

Mr. Gudgeons had, by this time, become a good deal more

passive, though he could not yet understand why everybody was not given into custody; and he got into the cab with Mr. Winks, and they both drove rapidly away. Dick Muzzle and the Doctor also went their way together; the former denoun-cing the two unruly Mudlarks in no very recordable terms; the latter bewailing the loss of the five pounds which he had advanced upon the security of the missing baby.

PART V.

THE eldest of the two Mudlarks had become an altered outcast, from the moment he had heard the doctor say that little Bessy Gudgeons, if properly managed, would produce from her parents the almost fabulous sum of a hundred pounds. He had never supposed a baby could be worth that amount to anybody, knowing how little his parents would give for him and his brother if they were lost. The money seemed so tempting—so inexhaustible—so much more capable than a score of good dogs, of producing stores of meat, potatoes, beer, and gin, that the eldest Mudlark confided in his brother, and together they resolved to attempt to procure the reward. What was meant by the phrase " if properly managed," they could not clearly understand, but they never doubted their power of making a bargain with the anxious parents, for restoring the lost child. The money, whatever they got, would be their own, without their having to share it with the doctor, or anybody else. They had stolen the child, therefore the child was theirs; why should the artful, comfortable doctor have any share in it? why should they not have it all? This was logic, though they had not learned it in the schools.

For the best part of three days they had exerted themselves, without success, to find the exact position of Mr. Gudgeons's house. They had a rather peculiar chart to guide them, which

they could not very easily trace. They saw so many dwellings,
each one of which might be the right one, that they were
rather embarrassed in their choice. As a chance of obtaining
a hundred pounds was not a thing to throw away upon a
mistake, they determined upon what appeared the only safe
method, that of retracing their steps over the same road they
had come the other night, or rather morning, with the child.
Having decided upon this plan, they watched their opportunity,
when their mother was out, took the child—which had been
left in their charge, and which was quietly sleeping in the
house of the late "black-nosed Billy"—wrapped it up in its
little blanket, as before, and with some food, which they judged
would be acceptable to all upon the journey, they went their
way unobserved.

A curious and a most unexpected way it was:—round the
dreary waste ground, along some wretched streets and alleys,
over a broad road, and up another street, which, from having
new and lofty but tenantless houses at the beginning, gradually
dwindled into a lane of boardings, plastered with staring
placards, ending at last in a long, broad, open, misty waste of
land, bounded by distant factories, and having many fag-ends
of streets running into it upon arches from the sides. It was
now nearly dark, but the two Mudlarks knew every inch of the
ground, and with sure, quick feet, and unshaken nerves, they
pushed on their way with the still sleeping child. Desert as
the place seemed, it was more familiar to the young outcasts
than their own home, and they felt an animal gratification as
they bounded over the hillocks, and along the edges of deep
pits, safe from any pursuit, if their flight had even been traced.
They stopped, at last, under some arches near the extremity of
one of those unformed, barely-outlined side-streets, that showed
little prospect of being warmed into life for half a century to
come. Here, feeling along the wall until he came to a loose
brick, the youngest Mudlark, who was not carrying the baby,

drew out an old bull's-eyed lantern, containing an oil-wick,
which he lighted with a match from a box he carried in his cap.
Passing again out of this arch, they kept along the line, with
the face of their lantern closed, until they came to the tenth
arch from the one where they first stopped. Entering this
archway, they went to its furthermost end, when, taking the
guard from their lantern, they removed some more loose bricks
from the bottom of the wall, until an opening was made large
enough for a thin boy to creep underneath. When they had
first discovered this opening in their wanderings, it was as they
made it now; the closing-in with loose bricks had been a pre-
caution suggested to keep it private, if possible, to themselves.
The youngest Mudlark first worked his way through this hole,
legs foremost, dropping into a place which just allowed his
small weasel face to peep through the hole. The sleeping baby
was pushed through to him, like a baking into an oven, and
the eldest Mudlark quickly followed with the lantern, closing
up the hole with the bricks, which had been placed within his
reach. Leaving the baby in the arms of his brother, he kept
the lantern, and went on first to light and direct the way.

There was nothing wonderful—as Mr. Gudgeons would have
said, if he had been there—in the place they were exploring,
and had often explored before. It was no magician's cave; no
passage leading to an enchanted castle—as Mr. Gudgeons
would have been delighted to find, if he had been there—but
simply a new, dry, unused branch sewer, leading into one of the
great mains that run down to the river. The two Mudlarks
had often been up these mains from the river entrance at low
water, searching for any treasures, in the shape of spoons and
forks that careless kitchen-maids might have washed down the
pipes. They were more familiar with the ebb and flow of the
tide, the floodings, the passages, the small veins and chief
arteries of this great underground system, than with the world
above. This was the hidden chart they had been trying to trace

back in their three days' endeavours on the surface to find Mr. Gudgeon's house. Along this dark and perilous route they had brought the unconscious infant on the morning of its disappearance from its father's comfortable dwelling; and they were now retracing their steps with the same burden, their minds full of the designs and hopes of children, their thin, weak bodies governed by the hearts and nerves of premature men.

Their course was not without many windings and passages to be selected, and it was some time before they came to the tunnel of the great main which they had to cross. The child still slept—the motion favouring its rest—and their attention was not therefore drawn from their route. Although they were on a high level from the river—although the sewer they were at present traversing had never been used, and was at some distance above the height which the water generally reached in the great main, the two Mudlarks noticed the very unusual circumstance of wet being under their feet. At last they reached the great main, which they knew they were approaching by the increased coldness and current of the air, and the loud gurgling sound of running water. When the eldest Mudlark came to the opening, he motioned his brother back, while he glanced up and down the huge, slimy tunnel, throwing his light on the top and down the opposite side, displaying the damp glistening walls, and measuring with his eye the depth of water at the bottom.

The survey was satisfactory, for placing the lamp on the edge of the brickwork, he went down on his chest, and allowed himself to slip gradually over, and drop into the water—nearly two feet deep—beneath. The baby was only got down by the youngest Mudlark leaning through into the tunnel, and dropping it into the outstretched arms of his brother. The motion shook it, although the eldest Mudlark, standing almost to his waist in water, carried round his arms with it as it fell, to break the jerk of its fall. It gave a few restless, whining cries,

but was soon hushed once more into silence. The youngest
Mudlark then dropped into the main sewer in the same way as
his brother, and the lantern was pulled down by a string which
hung attached to it, and dexterously caught, without shaking
out a drop of its oil.

Here, then, they were at last, in the broad, dark, echoing
main sewer, up to their waists in mud and water; two children
and an infant, the latter happily unconscious of its peculiar
position; the former fortunately being little men of the world
—the world beneath their feet. The two young Masters Gudgeons—as near as possible the same age as the two young
Mudlarks—would have been sorely put to it in the same situa-
tion; and yet, in the eyes of social reformers, the two former
boys would represent education; the two latter, dark, stunted
ignorance. Heart, courage, decision, will, nerves, self-reliance,
go for nought; the two Mudlarks would have been considered
ignorant, because they had learned nothing in the schools.

Walking along the side of the tunnel for some distance up
the sewer, with the moisture dropping on their heads, and on
the blanket in which the child was warmly bound, the two
Mudlarks at last stopped at a known mark on the wall, at which
point they crossed over the thick stream. The water in the
middle of the sewer was deeper than at the sides, though not
quite so thick; and the infant had to be carried on the head of
the eldest Mudlark, like a basket of fruit. When they had
effected the passage of this black river, they kept on their way
for some distance up the other side, until they came to a broad
opening, high up in the wall.

At this juncture, the hitherto amiable and passive Bessy
Gudgeons began to cry, and her nurse—the youngest Mudlark
—after rocking her to and fro in a very wild and excited fashion,
suggested an oyster-shell to amuse her, as he had seen a host
of infants amused for hours together upon the dismal waste in
Deadman's Fields. The eldest Mudlark thought food was the

best thing, and his judgment seemed to be right, for after stuffing her mouth with a piece of the bread they had brought with them, chewed into a pulpy ball, much larger than a full-sized walnut, the young lady for a time was pacified.

Poor Mr. Gudgeons, at this moment, was impatiently pacing the office of Mr. Winks, in a highly-fretful state of mind, listening for the messenger from Dick Muzzle, who, Mr. Winks predicted, would arrive long before the hour fixed on as the limit. If he could have seen the present position of his stolen child, there can be little doubt that his impatience would have developed into violent madness; and even the clever Mr. Winks would scarcely have known what course to take to effect the rescue of the lost little one.

The opening in the wall, before which the two Mudlarks had stopped, was the outlet of an old sewer, that had been disused for some years, the present active channels being constructed in another direction. To reach this opening, which was a necessary part of their journey, they went through a performance similar to that which had enabled them to gain the entrance of the new sewer on the other side, on the morning when they came through with the child. The young Mudlark, who held the infant, took up a firm position near the wall, and the eldest stepped first upon the calf of his leg, then on to his left hip, then on to his shoulders. The child was then conveyed carefully to the upper Mudlark, and when they felt themselves secure, the whole human fabric stood upright, like acrobats in the circus, with little Bessy Gudgeons at the top, the eldest Mudlark in the centre, the youngest Mudlark at the base. This position enabled them to reach the opening of the old sewer with ease; and the child was first safely deposited at the side —like a bundle upon an out-of-the-way shelf—then the upper Mudlark left his brother's shoulders, leaned on the edge of the sewer, grasping a hole made in the floor of the brickwork with both hands, while his legs hung over into the main tunnel; and,

finally, the lower Mudlark seized these legs with his hands, ran
up the wall like a cat, grasping his brother in his progress,
until he reached the top, and they were all safely landed in
the branch passage. Here again they noticed, as in the new
sewer on the other side, a quantity of wet and mud, which they
could not account for, the tunnel being generally dry.

Their road was now more broken and uneven, and more
winding and angular in its course. The child, having tasted
of food which was extremely unpalatable, went to sleep again,
perhaps in disgust at its treatment. The eldest Mudlark, who
still went on first with the lantern, threw the light, from time
to time, upon the roof and walls, showing how old the brickwork was, and how, in many places, it had fallen down, leaving
nothing at the sides but bare earth and clay. When they had
pursued this old tunnel for some distance, they came upon a
sudden and abrupt descent, which was not a constructed incline,
but a pit-caused by an underground landslip. To their right,
very high up, was a large gaping mouth of a main tunnel (now
also disused), leading direct on a dead level to the river, which
flowed at no great distance. So far, the two Mudlarks had explored no underground world that was not, or might not have
been, familiar to any other mudlarks of industry and perseve-
rance. But the two young outcast shad got a secret, and they
were not far from the place where the secret was carefully
concealed.

Nearly opposite the gaping mouth of the old main tunnel, at
the foot of the earthen wall—for brickwork it could no longer
be called—was a small depressed oval hole, neatly filled up by
the two Mudlarks with old rubbish and clay. When first made,
it was no doubt a rat-hole, and it had probably been gradually
washed out, larger and larger, by the action of the water when
it passed in and out of the old river sewer. This hole had
been discovered, almost in its present state, by the eldest Mudlark, when raking with his brother in the sewers, early on the

D

very night on which young Bessy Gudgeons disappeared; and
it was intimately connected with her mysterious abduction.
The eldest Mudlark—always of an animal, inquisitive turn of
mind—had, on that occasion, stooped down, putting his lantern
through first, and his head afterwards. He was not afraid of
rats, however large and fierce, for he had seen too many of them
from childhood upwards. He used to play with them like kit-
tens, in the days of his father's prosperity, when " black-nosed
Billy," the celebrated dog, was alive and fighting, and rats were
supplied in scores by Dick Muzzle, for matches amongst the
nobility and gentry. The light of the lantern, instead of reveal-
ing an ordinary rat-hole, showed the eldest Mudlark a passage
running in two slanting directions, right and left, and it was
not long before he wriggled himself through, his brother very
quickly following him. First they went to the left, but were
soon stopped by a barrier of earth, which had evidently blocked
up that outlet by falling in during some road-making, or other
similar operation, in the world above. Quickly retracing their
steps, they came to the point of starting, and then struck off in
the other direction. Here they went for some short distance
down a slight incline, and then up another slight and long incline, until they arrived at a dry earthen vault, the floor of
which was a soft gravelly sand. On one side only of this vault
there was a brick wall, seemingly very thick, and having a small
arched doorway, the door of which had broken from its rusty
hinges, worn with age, and had fallen on the floor of the vault.
Under this archway was a winding flight of narrow brick steps,
running up the centre of the wall, and ending on a small square
platform, two sides of which were still the wall, and the other
side (on the right of the steps as you ascended) was a thick
oaken partition, containing an iron handle, and secured with a
heavy iron bar.

There was the mystery explained of the stolen child. The
two Mudlarks, on their former visit, had removed this bar with

some little difficulty, and taking hold of the iron handle, they had found it governing a sliding panel, which moved easily and silently under the slightest touch. They had entered a large cupboard recess, and going through two doors, they found a large dark room (no other than Mr. Gudgeons's nursery), and by the light of the moon, which came through the old arched window, they discovered that it was furnished almost as scantily as their own humble home. Looking behind the curtains of the other recess (it was in the dead of night), they found Sarah Finch in a very heavy slumber, and the infant sleeping almost as soundly in the little iron cot by her side. It was the eldest Mudlark who gazed more particularly upon this picture; and the idea (which he afterwards developed to his father) came suddenly across his mind, that a baby must be a good deal more valuable to its possessors than a dog. It is true he had seen babies knocked and thrown about in Deadman's Fields, and dogs, too, for the matter of that; but this house was in another neighbourhood, wherever it happened to stand, and the eldest Mudlark, without further hesitation, stole the baby in its blanket. The young burglars, at that instant, fancying they heard a noise outside the room door, glided softly and quickly, with their bare feet, to their secret passage in the recess, closed the panel after them, and put up the bar with great exertion, retracing their steps in the same direction as they came.

This ancient portion of Mr. Gudgeons's family mansion had once been an honoured part of another spacious mansion, standing alone in the fields during those fine old troublesome times (entirely ignored by Mr. Gudgeons) when Charles I. was either king or recently had been. Down that narrow secret staircase in the wall, under that vault, and along that falling and rising passage, many an anxious wife or mother had conveyed some hunted Cavalier husband or son, while the furious Roundheads were battering at the outer gate. Now this historically-romantic passage, which in those days came up in a peaceful orchard, far

away across the fields, had had its ancient outlet rudely de-
stroyed by clumsy navigators forming a public road; while rats
had been busy in paving the way for mudlarks to turn its
venerable channel into the commonest of our common sewers.
The Roundheads and the Cavaliers had long been lying side by
side in their graves; but their places were supplied by two
youthful, muddy, book-ignorant, half-animal outcasts, winding
down the old passage with a stolen baby, into the regions of
dirt and filth.

The design of the two Mudlarks, in coming back over this
ground, had now taken shape and form. They had food, and a
light, if it should be found necessary to stop through the night.
The eldest, leaving the child in the care of his brother in the
vault, hoped to get through the panel, and thence unobserved
through the house, learning by this means, without dangerous
inquiries, the exact dwelling from which they had taken the
infant. Then his plan was, to come back and knock at the door
(which he hoped to do before the family retired to bed), make
an offer to the anxious parents to become the revealer of a
secret, and the restorer of the lost baby, and earn by this means
a handsome reward, punctually paid in advance. In the event
of foul play, which he did not apprehend, young as he was, he
had fully arranged the plan of escape. Only one person was
to be admitted to the nursery, and the door locked. The child
was then to be brought up at a given signal, and placed through
the panel in the recess cupboard, the doors of which were to be
closed, with him inside. Then, at another signal, the doors were
to be opened by the person admitted into the nursery, by which
time both he and his brother would have made their way along
the passage with the reward, and would have got through the
old rat-hole into the old network of sewers, where no one would
ever follow them, except outcasts like themselves.

This was the scheme—at once childlike, elaborate, and cou-
rageous.

It was now about nine o'clock at night, and they were safe with the child in the dry vault under Mr. Gudgeons's dwelling. Mr. Gudgeons and Mr. Winks were still seated in Mr. Winks's office ; the latter gentleman getting nervous, the former gentleman thoroughly out of temper.

PART VI.

MR. GUDGEONS's family mansion, since the peculiar robbery, was not like the same dwelling. Mr. Gudgeons was restless, forgetful of his pet domestic system, and constantly hovering about Mr. Winks's office. Mrs. Gudgeons had been taken nervously ill, and had been ordered by the family doctor to seek a change of scene. She had gone to stay with her mother. Sarah Finch was told to consider herself in custody, and she did so. She imprisoned herself in the servant's bed-room up-stairs, and she would not come down even to take her meals. She was heard to say, that bread and water were quite good enough for such as she, who had lost their character, and their master's and mistress's confidence.

The nursery was avoided by every one in the house, except the two Masters Gudgeons, and James Ross, the gardener and general man-servant. If Mr. Gudgeons could have heard one-half of the wonderful stories current in his household concerning this room, he would have committed arson, and burned the whole establishment to the ground.

If any two boys ever disgraced themselves and their father's careful teaching, they were undoubtedly the two Masters Gudgeons. The loss of their sister, after the first decent burst of affliction was over, had increased their appetite for the marvellous to such an extent, that their conduct was fearful to behold.

Nothing was too strong for them in the shape of romance ;

and they had inspired such rebellious confidence in the minds of the servants, that whole sets of ragged, saffron-coloured novels, written by walking nightmares, and illustrated by maniacs drawing from models on the rack, were brought boldly forth from clothes-chests where they had long been hidden, and read by flickering candles, bought out of the servants' own wages. Old hags of the forest, and unscrupulous counts with voices of thunder, had long fallen into deserved contempt; and the fiction stomach of the two boys especially was so cloyed with the wonderful and supernatural, that nothing short of a pickled vampire seemed capable of exciting their diseased palates.

On this particular evening, about eight o'clock (while Mr. Gudgeons was fuming in Mr. Winks's office, and the two Mudlarks were slinking up the sewers), James Ross, the man-servant, had brought home a book, lent him by a gentleman's coachman in the neighbourhood, and recommended to him as "a regular stunner."

"You see, Master Harry," said James to the eldest of his young masters, "it ain't got any o' them ghosts and demons in it, which we've heerd so much on lately, although it seems to 'ave; but hevery thing comes hout right at last, and turns hout to be a hold man who's bin playin' hup a nice game in a castle wi' trap doors, an' all that kind o' thing."

Master Harry (to whom the book was presented, as being generally the established reader to the group) did not seem at first to relish the description of the plot, but after a little persuasion he was prevailed upon to taste it. A fresh candle was set up, and they drew round the fire (they were in a kind of butler's pantry, a room on a level with the kitchen), Master Harry reading aloud, while Master Tom and James Ross listened.

The book was certainly not a literary production of which a nation might be proud; but its vices were vices of taste—its virtues were virtues of morality. The right man was *always* in the right place; the wrong man—nowhere. There was an army of characters, who came and went as they thought proper; there was incident piled on incident, without any tracts or sermons being artfully conveyed in the chapters; and there was an ingeniously-constructed castle that figured very prominently in the book, as full of mechanical tricks as a china-shop in a pantomime. Its title was "The Bleeding Baron of Barnet." Master Harry warmed up considerably as he got further into the story, and at last pronounced it to be "jolly and glorious."

They had been reading and listening, perhaps, for nearly an hour, when they came upon a passage that caused the eldest Master Gudgeons to pause: it was an elaborate and vivid description of a sliding-panel in the wall of an old oaken closet.

"Now, then!" said young Tom Gudgeons, impatiently—"what are you stopping for?"

"That's it!" said Master Harry, throwing down the book, and starting up, full of the value of a great discovery.

"What's the matter, Master Harry?" inquired James.

"That's it!" again shouted the eldest Master Gudgeons. "A sliding panel; that's how little Bessy was stolen; it's in the nursery!"

James could not believe that anything was ever built in a common house like it was in a romantic castle; and he endeavoured to persuade his young master against harbouring such an idea. But Master Harry had some little dash of the obstinacy—call it decision—of his father, and he would not read another line until a full examination had been made of the walls, and particularly of the old recesses in the nursery.

James was obedient, and not cowardly; and, getting a light and a stick, he went to the mysterious room, closely followed by the two boys.

At the exact moment when they were entering the nursery,

the eldest Mudlark, having made several attempts to get through the house without success, had got the secret panel open for the fourth time. He was about to step into the recess, and through the closed doors into the room, when he heard voices, and saw a light gleaming through the crevice. He had only just time to retire on the secret staircase, and hurriedly close the panel, when James Ross and the two Masters Gudgeons stood before the deceptive wall. If the eldest Mudlark had remained behind the panel, after he had closed it, he might have discovered a thin ray of light thrown across the secret staircase-landing, which would have shown his quick eye that something was wrong. But as he could not put up the iron bar by himself, without a struggle and a noise, and as the smothered cries of the stolen infant (who had been rather restless for the last half-hour) reached his sharp ears up the staircase, he went rapidly down into the vault. The two young Mudlarks had made a fatal mistake in their victualling department; they had brought bread for the child, and bread and cold potatoes for themselves, but they had entirely omitted the very necessary article of drink. No water was to be got where they were— the eldest Mudlark had searched the nursery above without finding any; and the child, they felt, must be crying for drink, as they began to be very thirsty themselves.

In closing the panel above thus hurriedly, an old cotton dress, belonging to the suspected Sarah Finch, which was hanging against the wall of the recess, had this time been caught in the secret door, leaving a thin line open all up the wainscoting, through which the ray of light from James Ross's candle was thrown on the landing at the secret side. This unusual crevice very quickly attracted the observation of the searchers, and a slanting push against the wainscoting, with a heavy pressure of the man-servant's strong hand, sent the secret door gliding to the very root of its hiding-place.

The delight of the two Masters Gudgeons at this discovery

knew no bounds; and if they had not been restrained by James Ross's prudence, they would have shouted so as to have alarmed the inmates of the vault, and the whole house besides.

James was not unused to underground work, for before he had entered the service of Mr. Gudgeons, he had been engaged with the company of which that gentleman was the secretary, and had had a good deal to do with the laying of gas or water-pipes. Taking off his boots, and grasping his thick stick in his hands, he left his candle behind him in the recess, in charge of the two Masters Gudgeons, and went silently and stealthily down the winding stairs. A sight met his eye when he got to the bottom which he had little expected. Crouched in a corner of the vault were the two Mudlarks, looking very muddy and ragged, the youngest with his back towards the wall, looking on, while the eldest was nursing the infant, and endeavouring to pacify it, as before, with pieces of chewed pulpy bread. There was a strong light thrown on its face, and on the whole group, by the rays of the bull's-eyed lantern. While James was making this observation, the two Masters Gudgeons above could not restrain their curiosity, and not being very expert or careful in coming steadily down a narrow flight of strange winding stairs in the dark, the foremost—Master Harry—made a slip, and fell, rolling upon James in a noisy and most unexpected manner. In an instant the two Mudlarks, with all their animal instincts aroused, were on their legs, and, with the lamp and the child, flying with sure and rapid feet down the passage towards the old sewer. James Ross hastened after them, but with much less speed, perhaps because he was without his boots; and they stood a fair chance of getting off once more with their burden. Their light died away in the distance, and the short, jerky cries of the lost baby, who was being excessively shaken in the flight, began to grow fainter and fainter to the pursuer's ears.

The two Masters Gudgeons were left in fear and wonder on

the secret stairs ; while the two young Mudlarks had got nearly to the bottom of the long incline which led to the vault. Here the eldest Mudlark, who now carried both baby and lantern, came suddenly to a full stop. The reason of this unexpected check was soon made manifest, for throwing the light down, and along the passage in front, they found it one narrow stream of deep black water. The eldest Mudlark had been warned of this flood by first feeling it on his feet, and the distant washing, gurgling sound soon told them the source of this unwelcome stream. The tides must have swollen during the last two days, and the river must have poured up the old main, across the old sewer, under the small hole into the secret passage, down the short incline into the low level, and partly up the long incline towards the vault. This accounted for the unusual wet and mud which they had found at the mouths of the old and new sewers, leading into the great main. The water, if not gaining on them where they stood, would be hours before it subsided, and the two poor Mudlark outcasts were caught in their own trap. They had no resource but to turn back sulkily, and meet anything that might happen to them ; and James Ross, to his astonishment, came suddenly upon the fugitives and made an easy capture.

When they were taken up the secret stairs into the house, they were looked upon as strange beings of another world. The servants gathered round them, and asked questions which they would not answer ; and the two Masters Gudgeons were particularly astonished at them, as no creatures of the kind were described in any of the romances. A messenger of joy was at once despatched for Mrs. Gudgeons. The child was carefully examined by every one in the house, and especially by Sarah Finch, who very properly came down from her garret, in all the pride of injured innocence. As Bessy Gudgeons, in her strange wanderings, had lost neither fingers, ears, nor toes ; as none of her limbs were broken or injured ; as she ate a good

supper of milk and pounded biscuit, and seemed all the better
for it; as she also took kindly to a warm bath and a clean
night-gown (for she was in rather a soiled condition), and
seemed all the better for them, the household began to look
with something very like pity upon the two poor, miserable,
doglike Mudlarks, who clung together on the floor in a corner
of the nursery, waiting for their doom. Food was given them,
which they did not refuse; and generally they were regarded
as two highly-curious specimens of the monkey tribe, caught
by James Ross, gardener and general man-servant, somewhere
in the bowels of the earth.

When Mrs. Gudgeons returned, she was delighted to regain
her baby; and after she had almost kissed it into a state of
scarlet fever, she had some feeling left in her large motherly
heart for the poor, wretched children who had stolen it, but
who had treated it well while stolen.

When Mr. Gudgeons returned from Mr. Winks's office, very
sulky and tired, about half-past ten o'clock, the scene in the
hall was nothing but a domestic riot. Everybody gathered
round him, without regard to age or position, and told the story
of the baby's recovery, all shouting at once.

Mr. Gudgeons was the victim of conflicting emotions. As a
father, he was glad that his child had been restored; as a man
of acknowledged business ability, he was annoyed that he had
not earned the credit of its recovery; as a respectable member
of society, he felt that he ought to give the two young Mudlarks into custody; as a man, he had some pity for their wild
and forlorn condition; and as a person with fixed opinions, and
a system of education, he was extremely disgusted to hear that
such a book had been brought into his house as the " Bleeding
Baron of Barnet," and read with such evident profit, as to lead
to the restoration of the lost baby.

Mr. Gudgeons, after listening to the story, which he extracted
with difficulty from the two Mudlarks, became more calm. He

was glad to find a reasonable and natural, if not a common-
place, explanation of the seeming mystery; and he was also
glad that he had got back his child, without acceding to the
extravagant demands of the irritating and extortionate Dick
Muzzle. Mr. Gudgeons delivered a long lecture to the two
Mudlarks upon the beauties of cleanliness, sobriety, arithmetic,
and the use of the globes; and as they listened very attentively,
he was so well satisfied, that in a moment of weakness he allowed
them to go. Mrs. Gudgeons, in another moment of weakness,
sent a servant after them with some money, the instant they
had left the house; but they fled like deer, upon getting their
liberty, and were never seen by the family again.

   After another lecture to his sons and the household, upon
the folly of believing in the wonderful and romantic, Mr.
Gudgeons gave the order to retire to rest.

   The next morning, Mr. Winks was duly paid for his not very
productive services, and Sarah Finch was handsomely rewarded
for the contempt of *habeas corpus* which had been shown in the
mild detention of her person.

   Report said, that she married the gardener and general man-
servant, James Ross, and was very careful with her own babies,
having them all tied at night to an alarum-bell, which rang up
the little household whenever they moved their arms or legs.
Report said, that Dick Muzzle became a shining example of a
converted thief (perhaps because he was not clever enough for
his business), and that his wife and his two sharp boys were
much improved by his reformation.

   Report did not say—for it was too well known—that in
exactly six months from the day of the singular robbery, Mr.
Gudgeons had removed to a house which he had had built by
contract, under his own eye, upon his own ground, far away
from Deadman's Fields, every brick, stone, and timber of which
was thoroughly and incontestibly modern.

AN ABSURD STORY.

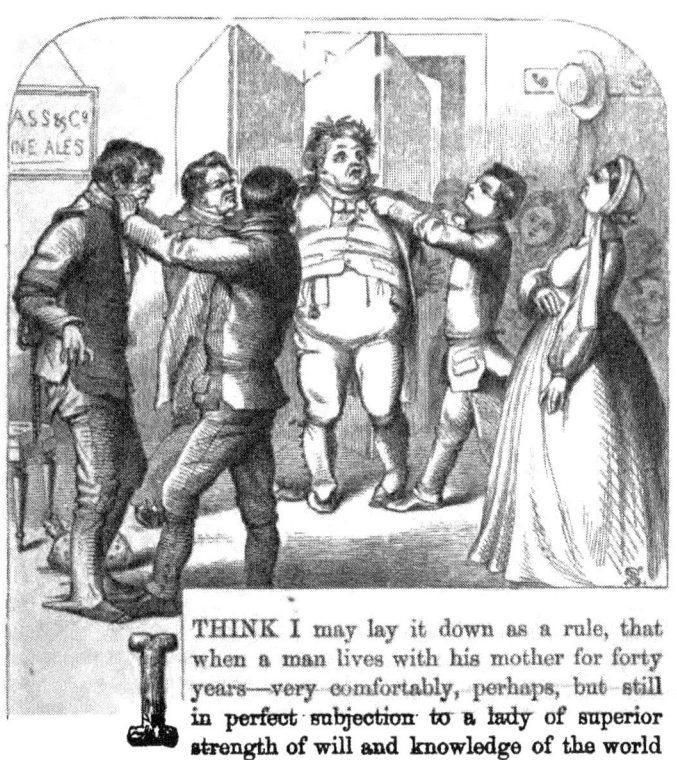

THINK I may lay it down as a rule, that when a man lives with his mother for forty years—very comfortably, perhaps, but still in perfect subjection to a lady of superior strength of will and knowledge of the world —all trouble of thinking and shifting for himself being taken off his shoulders, all his wants and wishes gratified so long as

he keeps within the maternal ken, and desires nothing that
the maternal judgment thinks unreasonable or improper, he is
not likely to be an individual of any very great force of character, or one whose natural and acquired powers are calculated
to conduct him unaided through any sudden difficulty.

Such an individual was Mr. Joseph Bowpot, the hero of my
story. His father had died when he was about fifteen, leaving
a tolerably good fortune, and a very good representative in the
person of his son. Mr. Bowpot, sen., was a husband who was
entirely governed by his wife; Mr. Joseph Bowpot was a son
who was entirely governed by his mother. The subject was
changed, but the ruler was the same.

Mr. Joseph Bowpot had all the appearance of a spoiled child
of forty; he was short, stout, dreamy in look, feeble in speech,
unintellectual in expression, with a small development of brain,
and a large development of cheeks. His dress was something
between the schoolboy and the ungainly quaker; it was chosen
by his mother.

However, notwithstanding the peculiar appearance of Mr.
Joseph Bowpot, and his perfect faith in, and reliance upon his
mother, he had a human heart beating in his bosom—a heart
that was as susceptible to the tender passion as any other heart
—perhaps more susceptible than many. Mr. Joseph Bowpot
was in love and engaged. The young lady (who, I need not
say, was approved of by his mother, otherwise he would not
have dared to think of her for a single moment), was a family
connection, a second cousin, or something of that kind, who
resided at Little Mildhampton, Salthamptonshire; and both
Joseph and his mother were invited to spend the Christmas
holidays at that very charming place, and with very charming
company.

They were to go down by rail on the morning of Christmas
Eve, and very busy preparations in the Bowpot mansion were
being made for their departure. These preparations were left

entirely to Mrs. Bowpot: Joseph was left undisturbed to his reflections.

Mr. Joseph Bowpot was very glad that they had been invited, as it gave him a chance of spending a month with his Amelia— a month of happiness, but not, he thought of undisturbed happiness; for he was conscious of his many social deficiencies. He would, in all probability, be asked to ride and shoot, and he had never fired a gun, or touched a horse in his life. Most assuredly he would be asked to sing, and he knew no songs; asked to dance, and he had not danced for twenty-five years, since he was at school; but what he feared worse than all, was the certainty, as his uncle was not alive, of being asked to carve, and take the head of the table. Of course, he never carved at home; and of all the defects in his education, this was the greatest.

Mr. Joseph Bowpot, though not a gentleman of brilliant ability, was not totally deficient in common-sense, and since his engagement to his cousin, a few weak germs of self-reliance had developed themselves. He had positively acted once or twice without consulting his mother; and he now, after much reflection, acted so again, by purchasing, unknown to her, a "Comic Warbler," a "Ball-room Guide," and "Miss Acton's Cookery-book, containing the whole Art of Carving." The "Comic Warbler" embraced the usual assortment of songs— some with bits of spoken composition stuck in between the verses—some with very bad spelling and transposed V's and W's, which were considered to be extremely funny, and others with choruses of inordinate length, in which "tooral-looral" was rather prominent. Joseph, after much deliberation, fixed upon the "Cork Leg," thinking it, no doubt, a novelty, and fancying that it suited his voice; and for many days the upper garret of the Bowpot mansion was made musical with its familiar chorus. This was the lightest task of the three; for mastering the mysteries of the "Ball-room Guide"—in which the different figures of the quadrilles were set forth almost as mysteriously as the stitches in a crochet-book—reminded him very forcibly of those days of Euclid that he thought had gone, never to return again. As to the art of carving, in Miss Acton's book, that was, indeed, a collection of inscrutable problems. Those were maddening diagrams of the hare, the rabbit, the duck, the pigeon, the fowl, the leg of mutton, the sirloin of beef, and the roast goose, all mapped out with lines and figures, like the plan of an estate belonging to a freehold land society, and with directions underneath as to where the fork was to be placed, and as to the course it was proper for the dissecting knife to take.

Mr. Joseph Bowpot devoted himself assiduously to his studies, but his progress was not very rapid; and by the time the morning of their departure—the morning of Christmas Eve—came round, he had very imperfectly committed to memory the words and tune of the "Cork Leg," the figures of "Payne's First Set," and some few diagrams in the art of carving—section, poultry; hopelessly mixing together the fowl, the duck, and the roast goose.

The time arrived to start; everything was in readiness under Mrs. Bowpot's guidance; the cab was at the door; the presents were put inside; the shawls and rugs were placed upon the seats; the bags and boxes were piled upon the roof; and Mrs. Bowpot and Joseph took their places, the latter attired in a rough travelling-suit, with wrappers and comforters, looking not unlike a member of Captain Parry's expedition to the North Pole. In about half an hour they arrived at the railway station, when Mrs. Bowpot, of course, fought out the battle of fares with the cabman, took the tickets for Little Mildhampton, saw the luggage labelled and placed in the van amidst all the din and bustle of a terminus the day before Christmas-day, and, finally, selected the carriage in which they were to travel. The bell rang, they took their places, the last basket of fish was tossed in, the doors were slammed to and locked, and with a grind, a screech, and a whistle, they were fairly on the road for Little Mildhampton.

On they went smoothly enough, stopping at very few stations; and, after the first twenty miles, Mrs. Bowpot, who, like her son, was of a full habit of body, and who was fatigued with the exertion of preparing for their departure, fell fast asleep in the comfortable compartment of their first-class carriage. Joseph's mind was too much occupied in revolving the comic song, the quadrille, and the carving, for him to think of sleep.

Joseph was always very regular with his meals—in fact, he was rather addicted to the pleasures of the table; and therefore, when the train arrived at the Swindleham station, about one o'clock in the day, and the guard announced that "ten minutes were allowed for refreshment," Joseph felt very much inclined to see what refreshment was to be had. Mrs. Bowpot still slept, and Joseph did not wake her, but stepping quietly over her rug-protected feet, he passed on to the platform, and through two sets of large swinging doors into the refreshment-room. Old as Mr. Joseph Bowpot was, this was his first railway journey of any length, and he was rather bewildered by the large room with its Turkey carpets, its mirrors and couches, its clatter of coffee-cups, and its semicircular counter, round which were a crowd of eager devourers, waited upon by a number of young ladies. After some little time he caught a waiter's eye; the waiter said "Soup?" and Joseph said, "Yes;" and he found himself sitting at a round table, with a basin of thick, brown, solid liquor, and the train standing before him outside the window. The soup being hot, it took Joseph some time to finish it; and when he had done, and had called the waiter to pay him, he noticed that the room was very quiet, the devourers had gone, and the young ladies had disappeared; nevertheless, the train was in the same position. He passed on to the platform, and there noticed a great stillness, very unlike what he

E

expected to find on the eve of the starting of an important
train. He looked into the carriages one after another to discover his mother, and, to his consternation, found them all
empty.

"What train be ye lookin' fur, sur?" inquired an intelligent
porter.

"Little Mildhampton," returned Joseph, rather nervously.

"No train till to-morrow marnin' at eight, sur."

"Well, but," exclaimed poor Joseph, in a state of nervous
alarm, "I've just left it—there's my luggage, and my mother,
and ——"

"Ah," rejoined the intelligent porter, "thee'st cum wrang
side; this be's Zummerset, that there's Salthamptonsheer."

It was too true. The unfortunate Bowpot had passed
through the refreshment-room to the wrong side, and had
fixed his unsophisticated gaze upon a train on another line of
rails, that was destined for a part of the country far removed
from that to which he wanted to go. His unconscious sleeping
mother was separated from her son—like Evangeline from her
lover—for the first time during a long and arduous career of
forty years; to wake in an agony of astonishment and terror,
in the middle of a tunnel or a deep cutting.

Mr. Joseph Bowpot—nervous, sensitive, and inexperienced
—thrown suddenly upon his own resources, was of course in a
very helpless state, and ready to be governed by any advice
that was offered him. Little Mildhampton being a small place,
it was too true that there would be no other train thither that
day; and on the intelligent porter suggesting that Joseph
should take a seat in the railway 'bus, and go down to the
hotel at Swindleham, he at once consented, and in a few
minutes found himself bumping along the country lanes towards
the town, in a very light, curious vehicle, licensed to carry
eight inside, but built only to carry four.

Swindleham is a place that has sprung into importance

within the last few years. It was one of the earliest towns to
throw off the spirit of the stage-coach, and to assume an aspect
of progress and activity. It built a new market-hall, a concert-
room, and two chapels; and the principal inn in the town,
which stood in the market-place, turned its large rambling
coach-yard into the assembly and billiard-rooms, and, with a
new front, abolished the old-fashioned title of "inn," and
dubbed itself the "Royal George Hotel."

It was to this magnificent structure that Mr. Joseph Bowpot
was bumped up the High-street, in a very uncomfortable frame
of mind, compounded of reproach for his adventurous stupidity
in losing his train—regret that Amelia, by living in the
country, had been the innocent cause of all this trouble—doubt
as to the propriety of his present course of action—and very
great fear as to how he should conduct himself at the hotel
until the morning. In the midst of his reflections, the bounding
'bus pulled up sharply at the door-step of the "Royal George
Hotel;" and to add to Joseph's discomfiture, he heard the
ringing of many bells, when there immediately appeared to
welcome the distinguished arrival a very stiff, clean, gentlemanly waiter—the incarnate representation of the new order
of things at the "hotel"—a chambermaid, and a "boots."
Joseph got out far from briskly, and his nervousness was somewhat increased when the "boots" asked him if his luggage
was to go up at once to a room. If he had had the boldness
then to state his real position, he would have avoided much
trouble and suspicion; but he allowed the opportunity to slip,
and was bowed into the coffee-room with impressive silence.
He sent out a shilling to pay the 'busman, and he had scarcely
got his outer comforter off, when it was indignantly returned
by that deeply-wronged personage, as being bad, or, as he
termed it, a "duffer." Joseph looked hard at it, and so did
the stiff waiter, and, what is more, the stiff waiter looked hard
at Joseph. Joseph threw it down upon the table, and although

E 2

it made a sound like a lump of putty, he thought it could not
be bad; but the "boots," who was waiting at the door to take
another coin in exchange, put it between his teeth and bit it
into two pieces, which settled the point as to its value.

When Joseph surveyed his appearance in the coffee-room
mirrors—the first chance he had ever had in his lifetime of
getting a fair view of himself—whatever his faith in the general
ability of his mother might have been, I think his belief was a
little shaken in her taste about masculine dress. The material
of his body garments was coarse and unsightly—being one
uniform colour, neither red, brown, nor yellow, but a mixture
of the three; this was called a "travelling suit," and, with a
long overcoat that reached to his heels, was cut in a style that
was considered smart when his late respected father was a
youth about town. The stiff, gentlemanly waiter seemed
paralysed as he gazed upon him; but he made no remarks,
and attended with dignity and silence to the duties of his
office. Mr. Joseph Bowpot, it is unnecessary to say, soon felt
in awe of that calm, cool, stiff, silent waiter.

"Have you any orders, sir, for dinner?" the stiff waiter
blandly inquired.

Joseph, as I have said before, was always ready for dinner;
it was his great meal; he watched for it, and he reserved himself for it. His love of eating would make him even adventurous for a time, as we saw at the railway station; and when
he heard from the stiff waiter that a splendid roast goose was
preparing, he threw off, for a moment, his nervousness and
timidity, and boldly ordered it in.

When this order had gone forth, the vision of his ignorance
of carving arose before him, and he rushed to the pocket of
his overcoat for the friendly volume of Acton, which he had
providentially placed there along with the "Ball-room Guide"
and the "Comic Warbler." Instead of sitting before the fire,
poring over the "Times" of the day before, and the county

paper, he turned to the familiar page (No. 48—article, Roast Goose, in the "Art of Carving"), and read up again for the forthcoming struggle.

While he was ruminating over the instructions, "Take your fork firmly in your left hand, and plant it securely in the figure 4," &c., looking at the diagram, and turning it about to ascertain at what part of the real bird the "figure 4" was likely to be, muttering all the while complaints of the unartistic character, and want of clearness in the drawings, the stiff waiter had silently laid the cloth on a table between the two bow-windows commanding a view of the market-place, and he now formally announced that dinner was ready.

Mr. Joseph Bowpot took his seat very slowly at the table, while the stiff waiter removed the cover from the smoking goose. Joseph made a great display in sharpening his knife, turning up the cuffs of his coat, afterwards his wristbands, then sharpening his knife again, trying it with his thumb, evidently waiting for the stiff waiter to leave the room.

It was half-past three o'clock, and being a wintry afternoon, it was getting dusk.

"Would you like the gas lighted, sir?" inquired the stiff waiter.

"Not at all—not at all," returned Joseph, hurriedly. "I— I don't think you need wait."

The stiff waiter took the hint, but he regarded Joseph with a peculiar expression—made up of curiosity, contempt, and suspicion.

Joseph looked carefully round the room, and finding that he was really alone, he drew the "Art of Carving" from his pocket, and opening it at page 48, he set it before him against the cruet-stand, reading it across the goose like a piece of music.

"Now," said Joseph, "'Take your fork firmly in your left hand;' so, (grasping his fork tightly). 'Plant it securely in

the figure 4.' That's about the figure 4, I think, (feeling for
the spot with his fingers). Very well; now to ' plant the
fork securely,' (trying to stick the fork in). Eh! What?
Why there's a confounded bone! Try a little on one side,
(shifts the fork). A bone there also. Why, hang it, it's all
bone! Stay, perhaps I've got the wrong side. Confound
these artists, I wish they'd draw better. It's no more like a
goose than I am! Suppose we turn over gently; wo! (Turns
the goose over tenderly.) There goes the gravy all over the
table and my trousers! (Sops it up with his pocket-hand-
kerchief, looking round once or twice anxiously at the door.)
Now then, once more; let's see; where were we? Oh, on
No. 4."

At this moment the stiff waiter appeared at the door. " I
beg your pardon, sir," he asked; " did you ring?"

" No, thankee, no," said Joseph confusedly; " I am getting
on nicely."

The stiff waiter retired.

" I wish that person would not be so officious," exclaimed
Joseph, rather pettishly; " he's quite put me out. Dear, dear,"
he continued piteously, " how cold the bird's getting. ' Plant
your fork firmly in 4.' (Sticks the fork in.) That's all right.
What's next? ' Draw your knife across from the point marked
6, through the figures 8 and 10, until you arrive at 12.' Halloo!
That's rather complicated! (Reads slowly, following the directions by corresponding actions with the knife.) ' Draw your
knife across'—So—this confounded knife won't cut—' through
the figures 8 and 10, until you arrive at 12.' That's about
here. (Stops the motion of his knife.) ' You then, by a
dexterous twist of the wrist, separate the leg from the body.'
(Pausing.) How dexterous twist? (Perplexed.) Somehow
like this, I suppose? Good gracious!" He braced himself
up for a great effort, but, unfortunately, instead of being successful, he twisted the goose off the table on to the floor between

his feet. For some reason, the stiff waiter again made his appearance.

"Ring, sir?" he inquired, more laconically than usual.

Joseph, in his trepidation, seized the dish cover, and clapped it on the empty dish, holding it down with his hand, while he turned round to the pertinacious, stiff waiter, and with something of indignation in his tone, replied:—

"I did not ring; I tell you I did *not* ring."

"Hem!" was the answer of the stiff waiter, as he again retired.

Joseph gradually recovered himself, took off the cover, and lifting the goose up tenderly with both hands from the floor, he placed it again upon the dish, and took a couple of glasses of sherry to fortify himself for a final effort.

"Oh, that extremely officious person!" he muttered to himself; "he has thrown me into a profuse perspiration. Dear me! the bird's as cold as a stone."

He took a couple more glasses of wine.

"I've not," he continued, "tasted substantial food for eight hours, and I feel the pangs of hunger. Why should I hesitate? No one observes me. I will."

He looked round, and finding himself unobserved, he tore off a leg with his hand, and hacked several small pieces off the surface, eating ravenously all the time. Cold as the bird was, he ate, or rather devoured, a fair quantity; and by the time his appetite was satisfied, the temporary courage inspired by his half-pint of sherry was exhausted along with the wine, and he relapsed into his original state of nervous excitement. Suddenly his eyes became fixed upon the dish.

"Good gracious!" he almost shrieked; "what a horrid spectacle! The goose don't look as if it had been carved; it looks as if it had been worried by a bull terrier!"

After reflecting for some moments, he continued:—

"It must never leave the room in that state. I'd rather burn it first. That wouldn't do either, because of the smell; I should have an engine here in five minutes. Good—a thought strikes me. I'll give it away to some one in the street, and perform an act of charity at this festive season. It's a pity to waste it; it shows the remains of a fine bird, even now."

Acting upon his resolve, Joseph went to the window and looked out. It was now quite dusk; the market-place was quiet, but a common-looking man, half tramp, half stable-lounger, who appeared as if he had not dined for some days, was walking up and down.

Joseph made several ineffectual attempts to catch his eye by nodding and beckoning.

"Now he sees me," he said. "I must break the offer to him gradually, or he may be alarmed, and raise the neighbourhood;" saying which, poor distracted Joseph sank despondingly into a chair by the window.

The individual—whom, for want of knowing his real name, I will call Smoucher—arrived at the window with wonderful alacrity, and looking through into the half-darkened room, touched his cap.

"Beg your pardon, sir," he said; "did you call me?"

"I did," replied Joseph, almost impressively.

"Did yer honour want yer samples taken round the town?"

"My what?"

"Yer samples," returned Smoucher, who evidently took Joseph for a commercial traveller bent upon business after dinner.

"No," replied Joseph, without understanding clearly what he meant; "that was not my object in calling you; I wished to inquire whether you had dined."

"Dined, sur!" returned Smoucher, in an incredulous tone; "yer poking fun at me. I never dines."

"Never dine!" exclaimed Joseph, in amazement; "can't you carve?"

"Can't I carve? Rather!—if I only gets suffin to carve; but mindin' gents' 'orses, and runnin' arrands, don't bring in anything werry strikin' for dinner worth speakin' on."

"Hum!" thought poor Joseph, "he can carve! Half-starved tramp as he is, yet is he superior to me with all my creature comforts. But, good gracious! that officious waiter may come into the room—I must bring this business to a close." Addressing himself to Smoucher, he said:—"Would you like a portion of roast goose?" adding faintly, "I've hardly touched it."

"A what, sur!" asked Smoucher, in astonishment.

"A roast goose."

"I should, indeed, sur," replied Smoucher, overcome, "and thankee kindly; I'm wery much obligated, I'm sure; an' if there's anything—"

"No thanks," interposed Joseph, decisively; "got anything to put it in?"

"Well, sur," said Smoucher, with some hesitation, "if you wouldn't mind my hankercher——"

"No."

Joseph took the handkerchief tenderly between his finger and thumb, as it was very old, and rather dirty. His excitement increased as he thought he heard the footsteps of the officious waiter in the passage; he hurried to the table, and hastily turned the contents of the dish—namely, the goose and a large gravy-spoon—into the handkerchief; glancing nervously all the while at the door, and scarce knowing what he was about, in the dusk and in his excessive trepidation.

Smoucher's feelings, during this brief interval, had evidently undergone a revulsion. He leant coolly on the window-sill, looking into the room, and remarked, almost loud enough for Joseph to hear him, "The gent must be cranky!"

Joseph returned to the window, and gave him the bundle, saying, "There—now go away, there's a good man!" But Smoucher, who had made up his mind that something was wrong, began to grow impertinent.

" Beg yer pardon, sur," he said, " but couldn't you throw in
a tater or two ? "

Joseph fetched several potatoes from the table, which he
hastily thrust into Smoucher's handkerchief,

" There," said Joseph, nervously ; " now be off."

" Beg yer pardon again, yer honour," continued the troublesome Smoucher, " but eatin' 's dry work, and I should like to
drink yer honour's 'elth at this 'ere festive season."

" There's sixpence—now go away," replied Joseph, his nervousness increasing, as he pushed Smoucher from the window.

" I shall never forget yer honour."

" No more !" shouted Joseph, in a frenzy ; and Smoucher
disappeared ; while Joseph sank exhausted against the window-
sill, like a sea-sick passenger near the bulwarks of a vessel.

The stiff waiter had entered the room, and lighted the gas,
before Joseph was aware of his hateful presence.   When Joseph
turned and saw him there, he sank in a chair near the window,
regarding him wildly, and still holding the sill with one hand.

" Take away, sir ? " asked the stiff waiter.

" Y-e-s," replied Joseph, in a faint and agitated voice; " take
away."

" Ain't you well, sir ? " inquired the stiff waiter, with un-
wonted tenderness.

" I feel a little qualmy—a slight attack of indigestion—that's
all."

· This was addressed to the stiff waiter, in answer to his inquiry ; but the words fell upon a listless ear.

That individual was standing transfixed with astonishment
before the empty dish that had contained the goose. Joseph
divined what was passing in his mind. He had hardly calculated the effect that the discovery of the disappearance of the
goose would have ; and his qualminess increased. The stiff
waiter was a man of few words, and he said nothing ; but his
look was awful—his stiffness seemed to increase ; and an attentive listener might have heard him say quietly, as he went out

of the door carrying the empty dish, " Well, if that ain't a case
of hapoplexy, this hotel's not the Royal George."

A more serious phase in Mr. Joseph Bowpot's dilemma now
developed itself. The fact had dawned upon him that he had
given away the silver gravy-spoon with the goose. Slight
symptoms of insanity began to show themselves ; he danced a
little, and said something about stealing a gravy spoon being
seven years; and that when his Amelia and his mother saw
him again, he would be a ticket-of-leave convict. When the
stiff waiter entered the room again, Joseph had calmed down
somewhat, and was making a considerable display of combing
his scanty hair before the mirror over the mantel-shelf.

The stiff waiter took a rapid survey of the apartment. As
he was going out with the rest of the dishes, he said to Joseph,
in his usual subdued manner—

" Take cheese, sir ?"

" Yes," replied Joseph, with affected calmness ; " I think I
will."

" A whole cheese, sir ?"

The sarcasm fell unheeded upon the ears of Joseph, who was
too much occupied with a sudden project that he had conceived
of getting out of the window, and scouring the town until he
found the man he had given the goose and the spoon to. He
felt the necessity of getting the spoon back at any cost. He
did not feel courage enough to go out of the door, and therefore
as soon as the stiff waiter's back was turned, he quickly slipped
on his great-coat, and with some little difficulty squeezed himself through the open window into the street, sacrificing one
of his braces in the struggle.

When the stiff waiter returned with the *whole* cheese—and
found the apartment empty—he was *not* surprised ; his suspi-
cions were merely confirmed. The strange appearance—the
strange behaviour—the bad shilling—the absence of luggage—
all were conclusive proofs in his mind of a deliberate attempt,

by an eccentric and accomplished swindler, to " do " the Royal
George Hotel. The notion he had once cherished, that Mr.
Joseph Bowpot was merely an excessively greedy visitor, who
devoured all before him, regardless of appearances or apoplectic
fits, now gave way to a strong belief that he was a swindler,
at least, if not something worse—perhaps a burglar! The
latter supposition was immediately confirmed by the entrance
of the mistress of the hotel—a stout, red-faced woman, of the
Mrs. Bowpot school—as most women are who are left widows
to manage hotels. The mistress of the Royal George was a
prompt woman of business, and without looking round the
room, or without any preamble, she at once said to the stiff
waiter :—

" Emmanuel, where's the silver gravy-spoon ? "

" Mim ? " said the stiff waiter, becoming at last very limp,
and looking nervously at the open window.

" The gravy-spoon ? " reiterated the decisive landlady in a
louder key.

" Didn't I bring it out, mim, with the dish ? " asked the now
very limp waiter, very faintly.

" No," was the prompt answer, like the blow of a hammer.

" Then," returned the limp waiter, looking hurriedly round
the room, " he's taken it ? "

" Who's taken it ? "

" The gent who was here just now ; a regular burglar, mim ;
he eat the whole goose, and now he's bolted with the plate."

" Ate a whole goose ? " asked the landlady, in utter astonishment.

" Bones and all, mim ; and he's gone out o' that window."

The conversation was here interrupted by the opening of the
coffee-room door, slowly and gently, and the appearance of
Smoucher entering timidly with his cap in one hand, and a
bundle in the other. Smoucher was not very well known in
the town ; for he had not been long down from London. The

landlady, however, recognised him as an idle, dirty fellow, lounging about the Swindleham streets, and the excited imagination of the limp waiter pictured him as another of the desperate gang in league with the suspected Joseph. The landlady also began, as she thought, to see a concerted scheme to rob the place, and this induced her to be cautious, and even polite, in addressing Smoucher, in the hope of discovering what the plot really was; while the limp waiter was marvelling much why he was not immediately sent to the Swindleham lock-up.

" What is it, my man ? " said the landlady, in an assumed cheerful tone, with courage on her lips, but fear in her heart.

" Beg yer pardon, mum," replied Smoucher, slowly advancing; " no offence, I hope; but is the short, stout party in, wot dined here ? "

" No, he's not, at present," returned the landlady, very charmingly, now fully convinced that an accomplice stood before her, who was not ripe yet for unmasking.

" Oh," said Smoucher, reflectively.

" Anything I can do for you ? " kindly inquired the landlady.

" No, thankee, mum," returned Smoucher, making a movement to leave the room. " I want to see the party myself on wery partickler bisness, and I'd better look in agen."

This would not have suited the views of the affable landlady, and she therefore begged that Smoucher would take a seat, while she sent a messenger to fetch the gentleman. As the fire looked very comfortable, Smoucher accepted the offer, although so much politeness made him suspicious. The limp waiter, under the directions of his mistress, handed him a chair, on which he seated himself, depositing his bundle carefully between his legs. The limp waiter made a motion to relieve him of his burden, which Smoucher decidedly resisted.

" Thankee," said he, rather doggedly; " yer wery kind and attentive. It'll do wery well where it is."

The waiter and the landlady having retired from the room

to concert operations, leaving the door well guarded by nearly all the servants in the house, Smoucher's object in returning to the hotel was then developed in a little soliloquy which he muttered to himself as he sat before the fire :—

"I wonder whether that rum gent knew he wropp'd up a great silver spoon along o' that goose? It don't strike me he did. Howsomever, there can't be any harm in bringing it back. If I kep' it, I might get into trouble, an' the gent may stan' half a sov. if he gets it back on the quiet. I wonder what he guv' me that goose for?"

These reflections were interrupted by a noise outside the coffee-room door, which now stood a little ajar, and the quick eye of Smoucher detected the servants on the watch.

"Now what *can* you mean?" thought Smoucher. "This looks to me wery like a plant. That party's surely never been a doin' anything wrong, and a draggin' o' me into the mess. Oh, unpossible! An' yet, what did he han' over that goose for? Bein' so precious lib'ral don't look wery serene! There's that blessed spoon, too. What a case it will be, if he comes in an' blabs out, with all that kit in the passage! This comes o' bein' honest."

At this moment the distracted Bowpot, who had been running all round the market-place, and up the High Street, without, of course, finding Smoucher, appeared at the window, very much out of breath. He could scarcely trust his eyes when he saw Smoucher sitting by the fire, and he exclaimed, in a very audible tone—

"That form!" This caused Smoucher to look round, which drew from Bowpot another exclamation—

"That face!" saying which, he struggled through the window.

"I'm blow'd if he ain't gettin' in at the window!" exclaimed the astonished Smoucher. "Oh, he must be cranky! He'll bust out about that spoon the wery first thing, an' I shall get lagged for petty larcency! I'll purtend not to know 'im."

Bowpot had by this time, at the sacrifice of a waistcoat-band, got safely through the window, and he now advanced joyously towards Smoucher, exclaiming breathlessly—

"Why, how long have you been here? I've been looking for you everywhere."

Smoucher, carrying out his determination, replied dubiously, "I don't think I ever see you afore, sur."

Bowpot, on hearing this, started back, crying aloud, "That face! I can't be mistaken—it must be!" Smoucher was getting very uneasy, as he saw the coffee-room door open wider and wider. Bowpot continued—"Where's the gravy-spoon?"

Smoucher made several mysterious pantomimic signs, saying, in a subdued tone—

"Don't be a blessed fool!"

"I a blessed fool!" shouted Bowpot, indignantly. "Don't make faces at me, you ungrateful fellow. Is that the return for the goose I gave you? I say again, Where's the gravy-spoon?"

"It's all up!" said Smoucher, resignedly.

Bowpot's eye had caught sight of Smoucher's bundle, and he rushed towards it, exclaiming—

"Ha! what do I see? I know that handkerchief—I know that pattern!" He seized the bundle, and squeezing it, said joyfully, "It's here!—I feel it! Yes; the gravy-spoon!"

He plucked the spoon out in triumph, threw the bundle again on the floor, and executed a feeble dance.

"There!" said Smoucher, sullenly, "now you've done it!"

This remark applied to a rush of servants that he saw coming through the door. The boots and the limp waiter made it their business to seize Mr. Joseph Bowpot; Smoucher was taken care of by an ostler and a stout stable-boy; while the mistress of the hotel, and a number of housemaids and chambermaids, made the background of the picture.

"Unhand me directly, sir," said Joseph to the limp waiter.

"What game d'ye call this?" coolly asked Smoucher.

A scene of tremendous excitement now took place. A boy was despatched down the town for the single constable and the handcuffs. Poor Bowpot, after the first struggle, became paralysed. One of the housemaids took up Smoucher's bundle, and the remains of the mangled goose fell out.

"The goose!" exclaimed the limp waiter.

"Lor!" chorused the women.

"How shamefully it's been treated," said the landlady, picking it up.

"The accursed bird!" faintly muttered Joseph.

"Oh! ain't he swearin'!" announced the boots to the company generally.

"There goes my supper," thought Smoucher.

The active ostler, boots, boys, and limp waiter began the precautionary task of bandaging the prisoners before the arrival of the town handcuffs.

"You're quite mistaken, you are indeed," said Joseph, appealingly; "I may be weak, but I am not guilty."

"I never see the gent afore to-day in my life," said Smoucher, "when he ——"

What Smoucher was about to state was interrupted by a noise outside the coffee-room door, and a powerful female voice was heard, exclaiming, in indignant tones—"Not a waiter; not a boots to take my luggage! Am I in a respectable hotel, or am I in a low pot-house!"

In that strong voice Bowpot heard the familiar tones of his mother; and although he felt somewhat ashamed of his position, he was relieved now of all fear of having to pass his Christmas Eve in the lock-up of Swindleham. Mrs. Bowpot entered the room with a dignified air that was unmistakeable. She knew her son was there, for the people at the station and the 'busman had told her so; but she was hardly prepared to find him with his arms bandaged with a table-cloth. At this moment the boy who had been sent for the constable returned, and, running past Mrs. Bowpot, exclaimed—" Oh, please, the constable's laid up wi' rheumatiz; but he's sent his little gal wi' the han'cuffs."

Mrs. Bowpot heard this, and she advanced to the shrinking, but immensely-relieved Joseph, speaking not so much to him as to the whole room—

" Handcuffs! Joseph! What means all this? Are you mad—or drunk—or what ? "

The landlady, impressed by Mrs. Bowpot, had ordered the bandages to be removed, and the unfortunate Joseph was now at liberty. He saw that an explanation was necessary, and he attempted one :—

" Respected parent, it is with feelings of the deepest humiliation that I appear before you in my present degraded position; but you're the innocent cause—my education's been neglected——"

" To the point at once, sir," replied the respected parent, sternly.

" I couldn't help it," continued Joseph, wanderingly. " I planted my fork firmly in '4'—I gave my wrist a dexterous twist—I——"

" Planted his fork firmly in four!" shouted his mother. " He hasn't injured any one? He hasn't committed murder ? "

Mrs. Bowpot's anxiety being relieved upon this point, and Joseph being evidently incapable, in his present depressed state, of giving anything like an explanation, Smoucher was left to clear up the mystery, and his own character at the same time, which he did as follows :—

" I was a-standin' in the market, a-waitin' for any job as might turn up, when I see that gent a-beckonin' o' me at the winder. Course I walks up; when he ses to me, ' Would you like a porshun o' rost goose ? '—them was his exact words— and I wasn't fool enough, o' course, to say no. Then he wrops

F

up the goose in my handkercher, an' along wi' it he wrops up
that wery spoon as all this blessed row's about. Course, when
I finds that out, I ses, that gent never meant to gie me that
spoon; so I brings it back, and sees the gent, and was about to
make it all right, when they 'as us both nailed for bu'glary."

This clear statement of Smoucher's satisfied all parties; and
the servants retired to the kitchen to laugh over the story,
while Joseph and his mother passed their Christmas Eve in a
"private room." There Joseph learned that his mother, as
soon as she awoke and found him missing, had, with her
usual decision of character, got out at the first station where
the train stopped; and finding upon inquiry of the guard, that
he must have been left behind at Swindleham, she took the
next train back to that station, and after a few further inquiries, had traced him to the Royal George Hotel.

The next morning early they started for Little Mildhampton,
where they safely arrived about lunch time; receiving a welcome all the heartier for their unexpected delay. Joseph had
seen the folly of being too reserved and timid; and warming
up round the fire in the company of his Amelia, he told the
story with great glee—although the laugh was often at his own
expense—of how narrowly he had escaped spending Christmas
Eve in the cage at Swindleham; and the difficulties he had
contended with in his first attempt to carve roast goose.

NOBODY'S CHILD.

S OME of us are old enough to remember a hot, close, misty summer—called the cholera summer—in which people stood in knots at street corners, and men went reluctantly to work, fearful when they returned of finding death within their households. Sad as this time was, yet it had its bright side, for many hearts were drawn closely together; much love, charity, and kindness sprang up in stony, barren places; many old hatreds were extinguished for ever, and many came out of the bitter trial wiser and better, because suffering, men.

In one of those smoky, pent-up London streets, where everything is dirty and cheerless, at the open doorway of a house were seated two persons, a man and a child. The child was a girl of seven or eight summers—if summers ever come and go in such a place—pale and sad, but beautiful and graceful even in her dirt and rags. Her companion was a middle-aged, bronzed, dusty, grizzly man—a wandering pedlar; and though many might have thought him repulsive as he sat there smoking his short, black pipe, the child looked upon him with other eyes.

Old Gipsy Jack, as he was called, was always a favourite with little Mary; now he had become something more—an adopted father. Little Mary's father and mother both died of the pestilence, and Gipsy Jack, with his wife and infant boy, might have died, too, like many others, had they not been on the tramp in Surrey at the time. When they returned, they found the little orphan crouching in the dark and filthy passage of the low lodging-house, ragged, miserable, and hungry—nobody's child. Gipsy Jack could neither read nor write: as to understanding workhouses, institutions, and such things, that was far above his poor powers. Many virtuous persons looked upon Gipsy Jack as a thief, which he certainly was not; but he was very poor—had often known what it was to be hungry, and miserable; and seeing a neighbour's child hungry and wretched, he knew of no other way of comforting it than of feeding it out of his own small store. Jack, with all his poverty, must indulge in the luxury of adopting a child; and little orphan Mary from that day became one of the old tramping pedlar's family.

Gipsy Jack had just returned from one of his solitary country rounds, and the child was happy, for she had watched for him for many days. He spoke to her of country lanes, of old farmhouses, of birds, of fields of waving corn, and forests thick with blackberries and wild flowers—spoke to her in his rough, rude tongue, but in no unkind way, and with his half-gipsy love of woods and fields, until her poor young, weary, yearning heart was full to overflowing, and her eyes were wet with tears.

"Let me go with you, Father Jack," said the little orphan, "let me go to those places you speak of, where those flowers come from that old Biddy here carries on her head. Will you, Father Jack? I can walk a long, long way without being tired."

Father Jack did not want much entreaty to persuade him. He never took kindly to cities at the best of times, merely putting into them from necessity, to replenish his pack, and being always glad to get away again.

The melancholy look of the streets now alarmed him, and shook his faith more than ever in the healthiness of towns.

"So thee shall, lass," said Father Jack, knocking the ashes out of his pipe; "go in and tell t' old 'oman to pack up the kit; we'll all get out o' this cholery bus'ness to-morrow."

The poor little orphan needed no second bidding. The dream of her young heart was about to be realised, she was going to see the country for the first time—was going to leave the black, stifling town, that had been to her so dreary a prison-house. She knew nothing of the hardships and privations she would have to undergo: she was a child, and dark and wretched as her life had been, she was hopeful and trusting.

Away they went at daybreak, a group much like many others who had gone before them. First of all trudged Father Jack with his pack and stick, his back bent forward, not from weakness, but long habit; behind him followed Mother Jack, a strong, stout, good-humoured looking Irishwoman, with her baby in her arms, crowing at little orphan Mary, who trotted at her side, with her little, earnest face peeping out from under a bonnet that covered her like a cloak, and with a dress that

looked as if it had been hastily made out of an old coat of
Father Jack's. A poorer family you could hardly meet with in
a day's walk, nor a happier one either; for the same kindness
of heart which led them to share their fare with little Mary,
made them contented with whatever befell them.

And so they trudged on, day after day, up dusty lanes, across
cool, green meadows, by the side of rivers, on turnpike roads
leading through simple villages and populous towns with busy
market-places; down again into the quiet country, through
arched forests, where the deer skipped across their path, and
where the child often lingered behind to pluck the flowers.
And when little Mary was tired, the pedlar took her on his
back; and at night they rested, sometimes in farmhouse-barns,
and sometimes in cottage beds.

Sometimes they had a wet day, and then they stayed in a
roadside alehouse, and little Mary watched through the dimmed
glass, and saw the heavy showers sweeping over the hills, or
played with her little foster-brother on the sanded floor. Sometimes, in their wanderings, they drew near the coast, and heard
the moaning of the sea at night. They saw the grass become
hay, and saw it cut and stacked; they saw the green corn
ripen, and saw it gathered in; they saw the leaves falling,
the days shorten into autumn, and the mists of winter creeping
on.

"Isn't it always summer, Father Jack, in the country?" said
little Mary, in a melancholy, inquiring tone.

"Noa, lass, and we mun 'gin to look arter winter quarters,"
returned the pedlar.

This answer made the child sad. She loved this roving
country life, although her little legs were always very weary at
night, and she feared now that they would return to the hard,
black city, whose hateful memory she had forgotten in the
bright summer days. But Father Jack had no idea of going
back to London. They were now in Dorsetshire, not far from

Bridport; and, to the child's great delight, she heard the pedlar settling with an old farmer for a little sheep-hut on one of the hills, about four miles from the town of Beaminster. This was to be their dwelling for the winter months—the pedlar intending to tramp in and out, on short journeys, with his wares. They took possession of their new habitation one November morning, and found it bleak and poor enough; but it was free and open, and they wished for nothing more. A large cupboard, filled with fresh hay, made a capital bedroom for little Mary; and it is doubtful whether she was not the most comfortably housed of the four. The pedlar started the next morning by himself to work round the villages, on his way to Southampton to replenish his stock. They stood on the edge of the moor, and watched him winding down the hill, and along the road, until his figure was lost amongst the trees.

Little orphan Mary played about the hills, in her large scarecrow bonnet and little jacket, with her foster-brother, who was just beginning to feel his legs. Many a fall and bruise they had, but they did not seem to mind them, and the exercise kept them warm on the frosty mornings, while Mother Jack went down into the town of Beaminster to buy their scanty provisions. Work of any kind was not to be had; capital was scarce, and the labour-market overstocked; and full-grown men, in bones, but wasted in flesh, were begging to be employed at a few pence a day. They all predicted a hard winter, and loitered about in a loose, listless way, doing nothing to soften it. The ratepayers began to complain, and the authorities at the workhouse commenced barricading their stronghold against the expected siege of misery and pauperism.

Mother Jack and little Mary, however, were not idle. Hearing that a large mansion was being constructed some miles off, Mother Jack trudged over to beg a load of firewood, and meeting some of her countrymen there, she staggered back with as much as she could carry. Little Mary's duty was to hunt about

the hedges for bramble sticks, and to gather dry brushwood
wherever she could find it; and so well did she execute her
task, with her little, rough, bleeding hands, that the old hut on
the moor was never without a cheerful glow in the evening.

Thus they lived on contentedly enough for many weeks, until
they began to wonder that Father Jack had not come back.
He was a fortnight behind the time he had fixed for his return,
and the small store that he had left, although they had hus-
banded it with great care, was now exhausted. One snowy,
windy night, having had little food during the day, they had
retired to rest earlier than usual, to sleep off the pangs of
hunger; but, although Mother Jack and the infant were in a
heavy slumber, little Mary could not close her eyes; for, young
as she was, she began to be conscious of a sense of dependence,
and reproached herself with taking away from the scanty store
of her foster-mother and brother. She wished she could labour
at some useful task, but she felt how weak and helpless she was,
and wept. Poor little orphan outcast! she dreamed not how
soon her young energies were to be tried, and her usefulness
weighed in the scale with gaunt misery, and not found wanting! She was startled from her reflections by a rustling sound
at the door, as if some one was rubbing against it, accompa-
nied by low moans of a person in pain. Little Mary had
nerves stronger than most children of her age, and although
her young heart beat fearfully, she did not cry, but raised herself on her straw bed, and looked out of her cupboard anxiously
at the door. She heard the click of the latch, and she saw the
door slowly open, and, by the dim light which came in from
the moor, she saw the stooping figure of a man standing in the
doorway, and creeping slowly into the hut. She then heard a
hoarse, weak voice uttering the name of Norah—the Christian
name of Mother Jack. A thought struck the child that it was
Father Jack returned, and, unable to control her excitement
any longer, and overcoming her fear, she started from her bed,

and clung to his legs, crying his name aloud till the old hut echoed again. This aroused Mother Jack, and, dark as the place was—for they had no candle—she at once recognised her husband. But how changed from the stout, cheerful pedlar who left the moor some two months back! Little Mary had kindled some of the brushwood in the grate, and, by its flickering light they saw before them a poor, faint, sickly, broken-spirited man, whose wasted body shrank within his garments, and whose hollow cheeks and sunken eyes, told a melancholy tale of fever and pain.

"Let me tumble into bed, lass," he said, in a husky voice; "I be ill—very ill."

They led him to the humble bed in the corner of the room, by the side of his sleeping child, and they sat up over the embers in the grate, waiting anxiously for the morning. The long night ended, and it came at last, and with it came the realisation of their worst fears. They gathered from him, at intervals, that he had reached Southampton—that he had slept at some poor lodging-house, used by the more humble and reckless class of sailors—that he had taken some fever, had sickened, and become delirious—that all his little property was spent, lost, wasted, or stolen—that when he returned to consciousness, he dragged himself away, and begged his way towards the moor—that, after pain, privation, and long suffering, he had reached his poor home, a broken, helpless, dying beggar. Yes, he was dying fast, and they had nothing to give him to comfort him. They were four miles from any help— and that help the union workhouse! There was but one course open; Mother Jack hastened down to the town of Beaminster, and applied for parish relief; and, after much anxious delay and cross-questioning, she got it—three coarse quartern loaves, and a bottle of physic, with a promise that the parish doctor, who had a very wide round, should look in some time in the course of the next day. When she got back, it was long after noon, and little Mary had acted in the meantime as a thoughtful little nurse. It mattered not, however, what they did, or what they brought—poor old Father Jack was beyond any earthly aid. He lingered on for some few hours, and died quietly, without murmur or complaint, about the middle of the night. When little orphan Mary rose the next morning, a new trial awaited her; she found her foster-father lying dead, and her foster-mother stricken with the fever—sick, listless, and unable to rise.

For hours and days little Mary sat nursing the infant, and watching by the side of her foster-mother, and still no doctor came. Their lonely hut was out of the reach of any cottages, and away from the road, and it was rare in the winter time for any one to pass near the place. Little Mary, with the desperate strength which hard necessity will give a child, dragged the poor, stiff body of her dead foster-father to the back of the hut, and laid it down on the cold, damp earth. How different was it now to that day in the black city, when he was strong, and kind, and loving, in his rough way, and she was lying, a poor, neglected, starving orphan, upon the lodging-house stairs!

Their bread was now exhausted, and the time had come round to go to the workhouse again; for they dispensed their charity there twice a-week, on a Wednesday and a Saturday. Little Mary disposed of the infant as safely as she could, and kissing her foster-mother, who became weaker every day, she fastened the door of the hut behind her, and ran off across the moor. Guiding herself by the church, which she saw in the distance amongst the trees, she reached the town in about two hours; and, once there, she was not long in finding her way to the workhouse. She was too early by some time, and she had to stand outside the building, with many others, who were waiting for the same bitter charity. It was a very dull, cold, biting day, and the wind and sleet, eddying round the work-house walls, cut into the very bones of the thinly-clad paupers who were crouching on the door-steps. A very miserable-looking group they were: women with children, children by themselves, old men, and lank agricultural labourers—hollow-eyed, heavy-looking men, staring into the dark future, and thinking of nothing but food, with their dirty yellow smock-frocks fluttering in the winter wind. At length the doors .opened. Some were admitted into the house, others were sent back, there being no more room for in-door paupers. Some took their loaves with eagerness, and slunk off down the town; others received their portions in sullen silence. Little Mary's turn came last, because she was diffident, and stood back. She told them of her foster-father's death, and her mother's illness, both of which facts were carefully entered in a book, and, with a promise that "it would be seen to," she was started off home with two loaves instead of three, one being withheld because of the death of her father. And so she went trotting along the hard lanes, and across the bare fields, with one loaf under each arm, scrambling through rough hedges, and toiling up the bleak hills, with her little, pale, sad, earnest face steadily set in one direction—that of the old hut upon the moor.

They sent and removed the body of her dead foster-father; and the parish doctor, an ill-paid, overworked man, administered some common drugs for the relief of her mother; but they seemed to have little effect, probably from the want of other and more necessary comforts, and the patient lingered on. Meanwhile, in all weather, hail, rain, or snow, on the appointed days, and at the same hours, was little Mary seen speeding through the mist across the moor to the workhouse gate, and toiling back again with the hard, coarse, welcome loaves under her little arms. One afternoon, near dusk, she ventured to try a bye-lane on her return, thinking to shorten her journey, and save a hill. She had not proceeded far, when she passed a low hovel on the roadside, at the door of which sat a haggard, grizzly, labouring man, upon a three-legged stool, with his face

resting moodily and savagely in his hands, and with his elbows
on his knees. It did not want a second glance, knowing the
state of the country, to tell that, in that hut, were misery,
starvation, and death. The man saw her pass, and eyed her
curiously. She hurried on. A thought seemed to strike him,
and he rose and followed her. His design was soon evident—
it was to rob her of the parish bread. She was near the end
of the lane, at the corner of the high road; and dreading to
return home without food, she clung tightly to the two wretched
loaves, for she felt that they were her life, and the lives of
those dear to her, who were anxiously awaiting her return.
There was a time, perhaps, when this man was kind and
thoughtful, and not the brutal savage he appeared now; but
misery and famine had made him desperate.

" Curse 'ee," he howled; " thee'd best gie 'em up, or by ——"
Heaven forgive him! He struck her a wild, fierce blow
across the mouth with his heavy fist, and she rolled bleeding
and senseless upon the ground. He had got his prize—his
two loaves covered with dirt and blood, and he slunk back like
a beast to his den.

The whole of that dreadful night the sick woman waited the
return of her foster-child, and her infant cried for his little
nurse and his daily bread, while little Mary lay stretched on
the roadside, bruised, parched, stupified, and weak from long
fasting and loss of blood. When morning came in the hut
upon the moor, the infant had ceased his wailing, and sunk to
sleep across his mother; his mother had sunk to sleep as well
—never to wake again in this world. If the cruel thought
haunted her last moments, that little Mary had wearied of her
helpless companions, and deserted them in their last need, that
clear knowledge which comes only with death must have taught
her how false were her doubts of her poor adopted child.

When morning came at the roadside where lay little Mary,
an old lady and a serving-man were bending over her; and

lifting her tenderly into a pony-chaise, they took her down into the town to a warm, neat, comfortable house, where they washed the blood and dirt from her poor little face, and having fed her with boiled milk, they put her to bed. Sending up to the hut upon the moor, they buried her foster-mother, and brought her little foster-brother back to life, and hope, and health.

Years afterwards, little orphan Mary had learned to read and write and sew, and had become a companion to the kind old lady, living in the town of Beaminster, in a brown gabled house, with an inscription on it let in on a crumbled stone— "Anno Domini, 1648." The boy, too, who had been sent to a school of charity at Exeter, had become a chorister in its ancient cathedral; and when his holidays came round, he always spent them with little Mary; walking over the moor in the long summer evenings, or sitting with their benefactress round the fire in the winter twilight, chanting lowly, in his rich, clear voice, that chant which the old lady loved:—

> "He hath exalted the humble and meek,
> And the rich he hath sent empty away."

WHAT IS A POUND?

A CURRENCY ALLEGORY.

T was a very dry job, indeed, and they were very dry people who were doing it. It always has been a dry job, within the memory of man, and there is every prospect that it will always continue so. It was not a discussion upon the Bank Charter; it was not a debate upon gold *versus* paper; it was not an attempt to answer the late Sir Robert Peel's enigma, "What is a pound?"—it was emptying a dust-bin.

The two men engaged in it were ordinary dustmen. They had had no advantages of early education, for ragged schools and like institutions were unknown when they were children, and their wits had not been sharpened by their work or their recreation. The first was monotonous; the second was beer. They were both about the same age—nearer fifty than forty—and they presented nearly the same appearance, though they were not precisely balanced in intellectual power. No two companions ever worked well together, or played well together, who were upon an exact equality in this respect. One man is born to be commanded, and another is born to command; and while the dependent individual seeks his leader, the leader, in his turn, is impelled to seek his follower.

This was the case with these two dustmen. The shortest was named Daisy, the tallest, old Crabshells; and what Daisy declared to be right, was so considered without any appeal, old Crabshells being only too happy to obey his companion.

Notwithstanding their ignorance, which was very hopeless, these men had a certain amount of philosophy about them connected with their trade. They had attained a thorough belief that everything is dust, and they had been suspected of allowing this belief to colour their work to such an extent, that walking-sticks, umbrellas, and even great-coats, it was thought, had been sometimes tossed into their vehicle, amongst the other rubbish, while these practical philosophers were labouring under this very interesting and curious mistake.

The task they had been engaged upon, on the present occasion, did not seem to promise much. They had been let in at a back-garden door, and let out again; they had seen nothing of a street-door, passage, or hall; they had neither been shown to refractory children, in order to tame and frighten them, nor had they had any opportunity of recommending themselves to the master of the house by taking care of his valuable wall-paper. The master of the house was unamiable and inaccessible.

When they sent in their humble request for the customary beer-money, they were coolly and temperately referred to a neighbouring drinking-fountain.

" Crabby," said Daisy, addressing old Crabshells in his usual familiar style, as they went slowly and discontentedly from the place, "when I works down 'ere agen, I spots that party's dust-bin, like a shot."

" 'Old 'ard," returned old Crabshells, mysteriously.

" How d'ye mean?" said Daisy, inquiringly.

" I've nobbled that," returned old Crabshells proudly, carefully showing a dirty yellow dump, like a brass button, which he passed to his companion.

" What's that?" asked Daisy, taking the article in his hand, and examining it curiously in the entrance of a court.

" Ah!" said his companion, "what is it? I picked it out of the party's dust-bin; that's all I know."

The two men turned the article over in their hands, without seeming to know exactly what it was they had gained. A little rubbing against their jacket-sleeves made it cleaner, and more like a tarnished sovereign than it was before, but it was still a mystery to them. Old Crabshells deferentially left the solution of the problem to the superior mind of Daisy; and Daisy looked as if he wished that nature had not been quite so lavish of mental endowments in his particular case.

" Blessed if I don't think it's a pound," said Daisy, undecidedly.

" A what?" asked old Crabshells.

" A pound," returned Daisy, with more decision: "you leave it to me."

Old Crabshells was only too happy to be led, even when so large a sum of money as a sovereign depended upon his vote of confidence: and Daisy began at once to merit the distinction which he had sought for and had gained. The cart was got rid of at the contractor's yard a little earlier in the afternoon than usual, and they proceeded, early on a long summer's evening, to gather the information of which they were in need. Their inquiries were not made amongst persons of their own class, as Daisy prided himself upon being too keen for that, and they went boldly into a large fancy stationer's shop in one of the leading thoroughfares.

Daisy had a peculiar method of gaining knowledge without exposing his ignorance, which might have been profitably imitated by much more important men. He was quite unable to "tell a clock," but yet no one knew this when he asked the time.

"Who'd 'a thought it 'ud bin all that 'ere ?" he was in the habit of saying, as he pointed to the taproom timepiece, when other persons were present; and, without having the slightest notion as to what he was pointing at, he never failed to obtain the reply he wanted.

This plan he had so often found successful, that he decided to try it on the fancy-stationer's shopman.

"Who'd 'a thought it 'ud bin all that 'ere ?" he said, as he laid the unknown coin on the counter.

"Eh ?" inquired the shopman, looking at both his strange visitors with curiosity and suspicion.

"All that 'ere," repeated Daisy.

"What, a pound ?" said the shopman, taking up the coin to examine it, and beginning to look for a customer when he found that it was a genuine sovereign.

"That's about the size of it," returned Daisy, now learning, for the first time, what the small property really was. Knowledge is power, but the knowledge that you possess a pound is a greater power still. They knew that a certain amount of good fortune had befallen them, but they had not the faintest idea what a change in their position this coin had already worked. Without it, they were nothing but two dirty, miserable dustmen; while, with it, they were able to command the attention of nearly all the world.

Everybody (in business) was sending in tenders for this
pound. Every blank wall in London, Dublin, and Glasgow was
covered with glaring placards appealing to this pound. Why
had it been buried in the rubbish of a dust-bin so long, and
hidden from so many devoted admirers and friends? Had it
bruised its oats yet? was a constant and not altogether disinterested cry. Did it double up its perambulator? and, if not,
why not? Did it wish to get rid of grey hair, or preserve its
complexion from the ravages of a burning sun? Did it suffer
from toothache, or from nervous pains in the head? Had it
tried a particularly fine full-flavoured congou—the only genuine
article of its kind in the world—at three shillings and twopence
the pound? Would it like to go to Scarborough and back
(being allowed three days at the sea-side)? or would it secure a
baby-jumper, and immediately enjoy a happy home? Had it
insured its life against all accidents by rail, by flood, or by field?
Had it used a particular kind of sauce, a particular kind of
pickle, a particular kind of starch? and had it been careful, in
all cases, to see that the labels, if nothing else, were genuine?
Had it dressed itself in the only trouser that was considered
elegant? had it eaten the only dinner that was considered perfect and digestible?

Columns of newspaper type were drawn up in closely-printed
files to ask the pound these questions; illuminated indicators,
like fiery pagodas, were also asking them in the middle of the
Queen's highway; so were wooden-coated men in the gutter,
and large, rude letters, coarsely painted upon brick walls.
Lofty iron railway stations, as well as cool river bridges, covered
the pound with a broad span, seemingly with no other purpose
than to shout these questions from all sides, and even from the
roof. Small hollow sheds, that stood at the side of railways,
seemed to roar out these questions to every pound, as it hurried
past in its train, like wild beasts suddenly deprived of their
prey. Flocks of hand-bills fluttered like pigeons amongst

the houses; omnibuses ran from point to point; pantomimic scenery was pushed on to theatrical stages; magazine covers attended upon literature; the very pavement under our feet became eloquent in words, and all for the same purpose—to address this pound. What is a pound, indeed? What is it not?

The two dustmen, as I have said before, were only very dimly aware of the importance they had suddenly acquired as the masters of this wonderful coin, for neither old Crabshells nor Daisy was able to read. Ignorant as they were, however, they were not wholly blind to their power, and Daisy, especially, began to grow authoritatively genteel.

" 'Ow fur, now, would that go in your line?" he asked of the fancy-stationer's shopman.

"How much can we give you for a pound, you mean?" inquired that individual.

"Ah!" replied Daisy, "now you've hit it."

"Well," returned the shopman, taking a pencil and some paper, and unconsciously assuming the ordinary tone of his calling, "there's our elegant album at three shillings, our graceful fan at half-a-crown, our cheap and durable inkstand at the same money, and our marvellous writing-case at two shillings, containing two dozen sheets of paper, two dozen adhesive envelopes, pencil, metal pen-case, with pens and blotting-book."

"Good," observed Daisy, looking at old Crabshells, as the shopman paused.

"Three and five is eight, and two is ten," continued the shopman, "or one-half, which you can give, if you like, to your good lady; while, for the other ten shillings, we can sell you a dressing-pouch, fitted up with every necessary for the toilet; or you can have a reliable letter-scale at two-and-six, a Russia or Morocco pocket-book at the same money, a scent-bottle at the same money again, a paper-knife at one-and-sixpence, and a *porte-monnaie* at a shilling;—that will make the pound."

"Eh?" replied Daisy, addressing old Crabshells, "what d'ye think?"

"Well," returned the inferior dustman, vaguely, "you know me."

"'Ad ought to, Crabby," was the confidential reply.

"Ah!" was responded again.

"We'll think it over, mate," said Daisy, this time addressing the shopman, "an' work roun' 'ere agen."

Once out of the fancy-stationer's shop, they consulted as to what they should do with their pound; and they decided, at last, to make further inquiry respecting its purchasing capability. Their work and their experience had never brought them into communication with any coin of the realm that was higher in value than half-a-crown, and they were naturally suspicious, and fearful of being imposed upon.

"That party may be all right," said Daisy, alluding to the fancy-stationer's shopman, "an' he may not. Eh, Crabby?"

"Right," replied the inferior dustman.

They went into a shop which was at one and the same time an heraldic office, a geological studio, and a copperplate and seal engraver's.

"'Ow fur; now, might that go in your line?" again asked Daisy, placing the coin much more carefully on the counter than he did in the fancy stationer's shop.

"In which line?" asked the shopman, willing to humour his odd-looking customers.

"All on 'em," said Daisy, "if there's a whole kit."

"Well," continued the shopman, smiling, while an old gentleman in spectacles was looking at them from an inner room, over a green blind; "there's tracing family arms, and making a sketch of them, that's two-and-sixpence; tracing pedigrees and family histories is extra; engraving crest-plate is five shillings; a linen-marking initial-plate is one shilling, a name-plate and a set of moveable numbers, for the same purpose, are two-and-sixpence each; and you can have another steel crest-die, for stamping note-paper, or a plate with about one hundred and seventy superfine wedding or visiting cards, which will make up the pound."

The two bewildered dustmen got out of this shop very quickly.

" I couldn't make it out," said old Crabshells.

" No," returned Daisy, " it even got over me."

They pursued their investigations, and the next shop they went into was a silversmith, cutler, and ironmonger's, where they asked the same question, in the same manner, and were treated with almost chilling neglect.

" We can give you plenty of things for a pound," said a stout shopman, standing guard over a large group of plated teapots, coffeepots, jugs, and sugar-basins, that looked like a brood of Cochin-China fowls; " but you don't want to buy."

" Is that 'ere a pound," said Daisy, pointing to the coin upon the counter, " or ain't it not ? "

" It is," replied the stout shopman, rather sulkily.

" Wery well, then," returned Daisy, " don't I mean the thing that's right ? "

" I don't know," was the reply; " I can't waste much time about it. Is it kitchen ? "

" Kinchen ? "

" Kitchen—kitchen ! articles for the kitchen ? "

" Anything yer like," said Daisy.

" Look here, then," said the stout shopman, rapidly turning over a list of prices. " Can you read ? "

" Not as I'm aware on," replied Daisy.

" I thought not," was the remark, " and I must do it for you. You can have a strong, useful teakettle for three shillings, a teapot for another three, a candlestick for a shilling, three spoons for ninepence, a fryingpan for a shilling, two iron saucepans for three-and-ninepence, a coal-shovel for half-a-crown, six knives and forks for four shillings, and a pepperbox and a dustpan for a shilling more, which makes the pound."

Having ascertained that more than forty such lists, either longer or shorter, according to the articles, could be made up at a pound each, if required, the two dustmen found no difficulty in leaving the shop without making a purchase, the stout shopman being only too glad to get rid of them.

They were not satisfied yet, and in a few minutes more they were standing at the counter of a furnishing glass-shop. It was a storehouse that ought to have been opened as an exhibition. If they had paid a shilling for admission, they could scarcely have grumbled, although so many similar halls of enchantment were open throughout London, perfectly free. Every shelf was filled with crystal bottles and goblets, or plates that looked like pictures; the roof was rich with sparkling, jewelled fruit, and the gleams of sunset, which came in at the back, were reflected in a hundred glistening mirrors.

The master, who was walking up and down the shop, was an affable man, who believed in the progress of the lower orders, and the great improvement which had taken place in their taste under the beneficial influence of art-exhibitions and schools of design.

"Ah!" he said, upon being made acquainted with their business, "a pound's worth? very good—very good indeed. What shall we say, gentlemen, quantity or quality?"

"A little o' both," replied Daisy.

"Good again," returned the china and glass dealer, "good again! I think our No. 8 blue-edged china breakfast-service of twenty-three pieces—six bowls and saucers, six plates, two bread-and-butter plates, one milk-jug, one slop-basin, and one sugar-basin—which we sell at thirteen shillings and sixpence, with a claret-jug at four shillings (which will do very well for beer, and create quite a sensation when you take it to your public-house), and a glass dessert-dish at half-a-crown, which will do for cheese, will make a very good pound's worth, according to my idea."

The two dustmen, however, were not caught, even by the

display of "our No. 8," and its adjuncts. They were very
difficult to please, and very suspicious. The affability of the
glass-dealer filled them with even more distrust than the
taciturnity of the ironmonger's shopman; while the more
articles and shops they saw, the more they seemed inclined
to see.

They found their way, after this, into a large haberdasher's
shop, that was chiefly devoted to the sale of ladies' apparel.
Their usual request to know what they could have for a pound
was received with considerable mirth by, at least, half-a-dozen
shopmen. Two young men were making faces behind a pile of
rolled alpacas, while two more were pretending to be busy in
arranging ribbon-boxes upon shelves. The two who had the
courage to face the dustmen, seemed totally unable to use their
tongues or their hands.

"Now then!" said Daisy, who became impatient under this
staring and tittering.

"So I think," followed old Crabshells, who, on this occasion,
gave a sign of his existence.

The first remark produced a burst of laughter from behind
the alpacas, which was quickly followed by a hearty response
from the two young men at the ribbon-boxes; and when the
second remark was heard, the two prim gentlemen behind the
counter could restrain themselves no longer; and, finally, the
whole six joined in one general shout.

"What is this?" said a tall, severe man, in a tall, severe
cravat—the shop-walker of the house—who came suddenly
upon the group from another department. "Are gentlemen to
be treated in this way when they visit our establishment? Do
we take down our shutters every morning on purpose to play?"

The allusion to "gentlemen" produced an undertoned repe-
tition of the word from one of the young men.

"I said gentlemen, Mr. Topham," repeated the shop-walker,
as he caught the sound and the speaker, "and I say it again.

Every person is a gentleman who comes to this establishment with ready money."

This assertion and reproof had the effect of restoring, to some extent, the proper attention to business, and the two dustmen were made acquainted with the cost and mystery of a lady's dress. There was a printed muslin frock at nine-and-ninepence (warranted our best washing fast colour), sufficient lining for the same for eightpence-halfpenny, a delicate waist-band for ninepence, a smart little bonnet-shape for two shillings and elevenpence, the ribbon for the same for half-a-crown, a sprig or two of artificial flowers for ninepence, a gauzy veil for eightpence-threefarthings, a bewitching cap at twopence-three-farthings, and a pair of neat little lavender gloves for one-and-sixpence. That was a pound's worth, and a very good pound's worth, too.

" Sir," said Daisy, advancing to the stiff shop-walker, " I respect yer, an' yer shall 'ear from me agen."

" Mr. Topham," said the stiff shop-walker, severely, address-ing one of the young men, as Daisy and old Crabshells left the place, " you've hurt the feelings of a ready-money customer, and the house shall certainly hear of it to-morrow morning."

The wandering dustmen went from the haberdasher's direct to a large tea-merchant's, where they learnt that their pound was not a whit less respected as a powerful instrument of exchange. They found that they had a choice, in black tea alone, of Lapsing Souchong, Assam Pekoe Souchong, rare Ankoi Souchong, Flowery Pekoe, Howqua's mixture, Melville mixture, Scented Caper, Padrae tea, and Oolong Souchong. The green teas, the coffees, the cocoas, the chocolates, the spices, fruits, and sugars, were almost endless in their variety ; and it seemed as if the whole world had been ransacked to find a worthy pound's worth for these two common dustmen. There was half-a-pound of strong black useful Congou for one shilling and sixpence, half-a-pound of green Twankey for one shilling and fourpence, one pound of Ceylon coffee for one shilling, one pound of old English mustard for sixpence, one pound of arrowroot for eightpence, another pound of tapioca for sevenpence, a pound of maccaroni for sixpence, one pound of Carolina rice for fivepence, one pound of Cephalonia currants for fourpence, one pound of Valencia raisins for fivepence, one pound of Eleme figs for sevenpence, one pound of imperial French plums for eightpence, one pound of Tafilat dates for a shilling, one pound of Normandy pippins for fivepence, one pound of Jordan almonds for one shilling and sixpence, one pound of citron for one shilling, one pound of cinnamon for three shillings, one pound of sago for threepence, one pound of pepper for one shilling and twopence, one pound of carraway seeds for sixpence, one pound of roll cocoa at one shilling and fourpence, and one pound of Sir H. Sloane's chocolate for the same money;—making twenty-one pounds of fragrant produce, in exchange for a pound in money.

From the tea-merchant's these two inquiring dustmen wandered into the shop of a cheap tailor, to see if their pound would procure a suit of clothes of a gay and gentlemanly character.

" Put you into a suit for a pound ?" said a smart, off-hand shopman; " I should think we could! Make you an ornament to your country!"

The two dustmen exchanged signs of approval.

" There," continued the shopman, exhibiting a light Holland morning coat at three shillings and sixpence, a pair of tweed trousers at eight-and-sixpence, a quilting waistcoat at six-and-sixpence, and a fancy neck-tie at eighteenpence. " There, look at that! Take her to St. George's, Hanover-square, and they wouldn't know you!"

" How d'ye mean ?" asked Daisy.

" Oh, you know fast enough," returned the shopman, jocularly; " going to get spliced; quite right. Now, I tell you what I'll do with you——"

He broke off at this point, observing that Daisy and his
companion were examining the strength of the trousers.

"Ah, you may pull 'em," he continued; "you may pull 'em.
You don't know the Marquis of Waterford?"

"Me and my mate 'ull talk it hover," said Daisy, leaving the
shop with his companion.

"Now, look here!" said the shopman, vaulting over the
counter, and running after them to the door; "I tell you what
I'll do with you—I want to deal: I'll throw in a shirt, though
I don't get a penny by you."

Observing that this liberal offer was not accepted, he asked
them, in a loud tone, "if eighteen shillings would break their
backs?" but they still continued on their way.

They went into a bedding upholsterer's warehouse next, most
probably because they began to feel tired; and they found that
their pound was still respected, although much more limited in
its power of purchase. They were waited on by a mild-eyed,
small, thin, middle-aged man, with a pen behind his ear, who
rubbed his hands, and did not seem astonished at the peculiar
appearance of his customers.

"There's our reeded swing cedar toilet-glass," he said, "at
five shillings, which, with five of our white beach caned-bot-
tomed chairs at three shillings each, will make one pound's
worth. There is our folding Derby birch chair (cane back and
seat) at thirteen shillings, which, with a toilet-service at four-
and-six, and a hanging looking-glass at half-a-crown, will make
another pound's worth. There is our three-feet-by-six portable
folding iron bedstead, which comes to exactly one pound; or
there is our deal toilet-table—a very useful article for general
common wear—at seven shillings, our deal washstand with
drawers, at seven-and-sixpence, our deal towel-horse at three
shillings, which, with the half-crown looking-glass before mentioned, will make another excellent pound's worth. We can
give you a good serviceable mattress for nine shillings, and

one pair of nine-quarter blankets for eleven shillings, which
will make another pound's worth. We really ought to say
eleven-and-sixpence for these last articles, but I suppose we
must only charge eleven to you."

Judging from the tone and manner with which the last two
words of this sentence were given, any hearer would have supposed that "the house," through its representative, had suddenly taken a particular fancy to the two dustmen.

"Ain't you got nothink cheaper than them 'ere ?" asked
Daisy, "anythink in the heasy chair line ?"

"No," replied the little man, very mildly, "we keep nothing
but the best—the very best."

As they were leaving this place in search of another shop, a
sudden idea seemed to have come into the mind of old Crabshells.

"Daisy," he said, "ain't we 'ad enough o' this ?"

"Well," returned Daisy, cautiously, "I don't know."

"'Ow about supper an' a drink ?" asked old Crabshells.

"You knows a thing or two, Cocky, don't you ?" was the
reply. The two dustmen looked admiringly at each other, and
went into the first tavern they found upon the road.

After two quarts of beer, which came to eightpence, two
basins of soup at tenpence each, a rumpsteak at a shilling, a
couple of pork-chops at ninepence each, and six small loaves
which came to sixpence, they began to grow dainty.

"Crabby," said Daisy, "'ow d'ye feel ?"

"Dry," replied old Crabshells.

"Crabby," said Daisy, picking his teeth with a fork, "we'll
go it."

"Daisy," replied old Crabshells, leaning across the table of
the box in which they were sitting, "you know me."

"Hi, mate !" said Daisy, calling the waiter; "what's that
stuff the gents drink when they're hout on the loose ?"

The waiter was attentive, though familiar; he had got the
pound in hand, and knew exactly how far it would go.

"Well," he replied, "there's port and sherry, but champagne is considered the correct thing."

"Oh, 'ang the c'rect thing," returned Daisy, "bring us a pot o' port."

"We don't draw it in mugs," said the waiter, timidly, "we sell it in bottles."

The bottle of port was ordered and brought, and turned into the mug which had held the beer.

"Eh?" said Daisy, taking a drink, and passing the mug to his friend, with an expression of disgust and disappointment on his face.

"I don't think much on that," replied old Crabshells, with a similar expression of face, after following his companion's example.

"Hi, mate!" again shouted Daisy to the waiter, who came at once; "what's that 'ere other stuff you spoke on?"

"Champagne."

"Bring us some o' that, then; we'll 'ave some 'arf-an-'arf."

The bottle of champagne—a nine-shilling bottle—was brought, and mixed with the remainder of the port-wine.

"That's more like beer," said Daisy, when he had tasted the mixture; "but I think it wants a little o' the right sort to gi' it another lift."

The waiter was again called, and it being found that another half-gallon of beer at eightpence would complete the pound's-worth of refreshment, that quantity of liquor was brought, and mixed with the tankard of wine. . . . . .

The last dregs of the novel punch were drained; the tavern lights were extinguished; the two sleepy, stupid, drunken men were guided out of the tavern door, and left to themselves and the friendly support of a neighbouring lamp-post. The spell was broken. The golden key—so easily found—that had opened the gates of knowledge, variety, and plenty, had as easily melted away. The pound was gone, and its late possessors were once more nothing but two dirty, miserable dustmen.

AN EARLY-CLOSING PROBLEM.

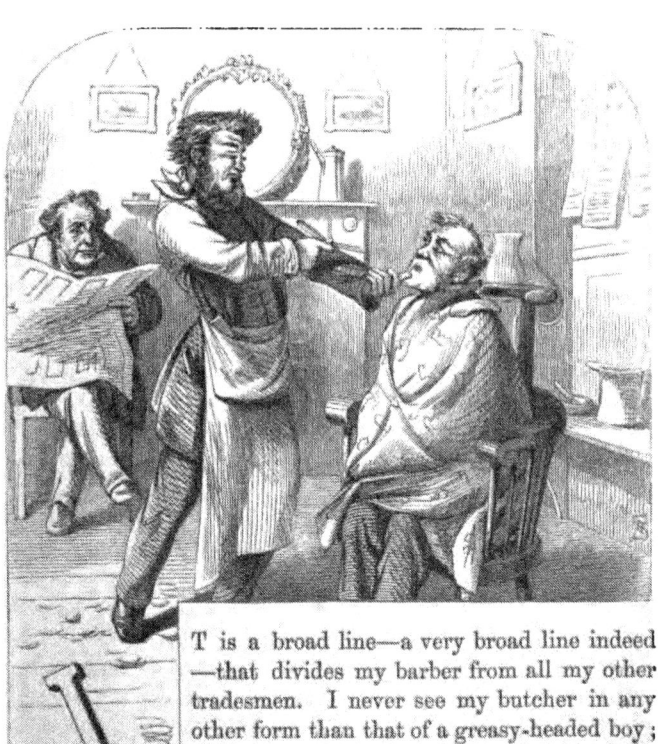

T is a broad line—a very broad line indeed —that divides my barber from all my other tradesmen. I never see my butcher in any other form than that of a greasy-headed boy; my baker may have gone to Australia on a speculative trip, or may have made a private and fraudulent transfer of his business; and my grocer may be, and is, I believe, a gentleman who buys pictures, and rides in his carriage. My tea and coffee come and go; my bread is light, and with not more than the usual allowance of alum; my meat is fresh; and I neither know nor care who provides these things, so long as they are fairly and punctually provided.

With far different eyes, however, do I look upon my barber. He is my barber, in the strictest sense of the term, by virtue of a confidence that has been years in growing to its present delightful maturity. No other barber is genuine. Not only has long habit made him familiar to me as a barber, and allowed me to place my face and throat in his hands without a misgiving, while he performs any up-strokes he thinks necessary with a sharp and glistening razor, but it has brought me into communion with him as a man and a friend—a friend with whom I have more unfettered, unreserved conversation in the course of a week, than with any one else, except my bosom intimates, in the course of a twelvemonth.

My barber is not an "artist," and his shop is neither a "saloon" nor a bazaar. His business is small, and it is the interest of his customers to keep it so. We wish him every prosperity, up to the point where he still will have no occasion to engage a deputy—but not beyond it. No man, for instance, would grieve more than myself, if I went, any morning, into his humble receiving-room, and found him quite unable to attend upon me in person, in consequence of the crowd of customers who were there before me. Few people care to be made the blocks upon which the crude apprentice or the unskilful workman is allowed to practice. It is one of the hidden mysteries of the barber's trade, as to where the men are obtained who are willing to be mangled for a consideration, and where they retire to between their disfigurement and their restoration.

Our neighbourhood is not calculated to produce any overwhelming amount of business for my barber, even under any possible condition of its future development. It is not a village,

and yet it is a village; it is not the metropolis, and yet it is
the metropolis. We join hands with the great centre of
English civilization, through a long succession of semi-detached
villas; we hear the hum of its restless traffic through the day;
we see its dotted golden lamps, like spangles, coming through
the mist at night, and the black dome of its huge cathedral
standing like an inverted goblet in the air.

My barber's shop was in existence before our suburb had
connected itself with the metropolis, and my barber has taken
no pains to alter its original features. A few flabby powder-
puffs, a small pyramid of pomatum-boxes, and a glass jar half-
full of tooth-brushes, constitute his chief window stock-in-trade.
Inside the shop we cannot boast of any luxurious fittings. A
circular looking-glass, the faded cast-away of some ancient
drawing-room; a common washhand-stand, on which is placed
the black and cinder-crusted shaving-pot; a deal table, on
which is a bruised block that always bears the false "front" of
some old lady in the neighbourhood, or the equally false
"back-hair" of some young one who is treading early in the
path of deception; a common shelf, on which is a pile of old
greasy black-handled razors; a few Windsor chairs; a newspaper, quite a week old; a long coarse jack-towel for the
common customers, and a few finer hand-towels for the aris-
tocracy, form the principal furniture of this humble establishment. The operating-seat, as we jocularly call it, is an old
horse-hair arm-chair that has been patched and mended a
hundred times. It is provided with a kind of crutch that is
fastened at the back, the cross-handle of which, well-covered
with leather, is made to fit into the hollow of each customer's
neck, and support him in one position, as in a photographer's
vice.

My barber, personally, is a little timid man, who is afraid
to leave his door-step for a moment (except on Sunday), for
fear he should disappoint a customer. He is a widower with

two children, a boy and a girl. The girl keeps his little household clean and tidy; but the boy is disorderly, fond of the streets, and will not be broken into the business. I never go out for a walk, but I think of my barber's close confinement. From eight o'clock in the morning, when he opens his shop, until eleven o'clock at night, when he closes it, he is constantly at his post, and he has had no holiday, on a working-day, to my knowledge, except one, for nearly fifteen years.

This one holiday originated with me, and I have good reason to remember it.

"Jones," I said, one day, to a neighbour with whom I am tolerably intimate, "I think poor Peebles, our barber, ought to have a holiday. He's nine-and-forty years of age, and it's high time that he saw the British Museum."

"Hasn't he ever seen that institution of our country?" asked Jones, in astonishment.

"Never," I replied; "nor yet a variety of other places, except from the outside. He never gets out except on Sunday."

"Ha! true," returned Jones; "I never thought of that; and when he speaks about them, then, he's only talking from hearsay?"

"Exactly."

"Dear me, how singular! But how do you propose to relieve him?"

"By engaging a deputy. A few of us can subscribe the money to pay for this, and all other incidental expenses; and if we tell him, firmly and authoritatively, that he must go out for a day, he'll not venture to disobey us."

A little further conversation with Mr. Jones and a few other gentlemen, customers of barber Peebles, soon settled the matter. A small sum of money was easily collected, and the man who had never seen the British Museum, and a variety of other places, was told one morning that a holiday had been prepared for him.

"Oh, thank you, gentlemen, much obliged, I'm sure," said the little barber, nervously; "but—but—oh, dear me! yes, I should like it very much, but it can't be done any way; it can't be done."

"Oh, yes, it can, Peebles," we said.

"Excuse me, gentlemen," he replied timidly, "excuse me; there's Mr. Stubble at the Grove, who never gets up till twelve o'clock in the day, and who wouldn't let any one shave him, except me, for fifty pounds; there's Mr. Dodo, the con-tractor ——"

"Peebles," we said, firmly, "we've arranged all this. You've been tantalised long enough by exhibiting bills referring to other people's excursions—High Hill Ferry, Hampton Court and back for three-and-sixpence, United Odd Fellows to South-end, and such-like diversions; and now it's your turn to have a day out."

"I'm much obliged to you for your kindness," he said; "but it'll only unsettle me; it will, indeed."

"Peebles," we said, conclusively, "we'll hear no more: you shall start next Wednesday."

The day we had fixed for little Peebles's holiday turned out to be remarkably fine, and the deputy we had hired for him, through a certain hair-merchant, turned out to be remarkably punctual.

The great difficulty was in getting little Peebles off. We had fortunately booked a place for him by the first omnibus to town, or I doubt very much whether, with all our weight of authority, we should ever have prevailed upon him to start. He was only going to be absent about twelve hours, and yet he left instructions enough with his two children to last a year. He looked very suspiciously at the man who was to take his place, and seemed to dread delivering up his flock to be sheared by the possibly incompetent stranger. There was little time left for doubt and hesitation. The omnibus-driver, according

H

to our directions, called for him at eight o'clock in the morning, at the shop door; and he was trotting away before he knew exactly where he was, looking wistfully backwards, instead of hopefully forwards, until the vehicle was out of sight.

The man we had engaged to take his place was stout and red-faced; off-hand in manner, and evidently fully impressed with a sense of his own skill. He knew he was only retained for a day, and he seemed to wish that every one should observe, within that short time, how vastly superior he was to the inferior Peebles, with whom the neighbourhood seemed so blindly satisfied. His style of sharpening razors had a touch of the juggler about it. He tossed the brushes about, as if, although clean, they were not ornamental enough to please him. He shrugged his shoulders at the jack-towel, whistled when he observed the looking-glass, and was quietly heard to say, with the intention of being overheard, " No heintment of the Druids ! an' he calls hisself a 'air-dresser."

I observed all this during the morning, while I was reading, or supposed to be reading, a newspaper; and towards mid-day I left him to himself, while I went to take my usual walk and my gossip at the reading-room of our literary institution. Much of little Peebles's business had been put off, by arrangement with the principal customers, and the run of shaving never took place until the latter part of the afternoon.

It was considered at the reading-room that, in order to encourage little Peebles when he came home, and pave the way for his taking a future holiday, we ought to exhibit sufficient confidence in the deputy we had provided, to allow him to shave us. Several of us who were in the habit of dining out, and who were rather particular about our personal appearance, really required shaving, and were totally unable to perform that very necessary operation upon ourselves.

Benjamin Franklin would have pitied us; for, from long dependence upon another, we had lost the use of our shaving hands. Others, who were not so particular about having a clean smooth face, could have waited very well until the next morning; but it was generally agreed that it was advisable to allow the barber's deputy to act in every way as if he was little Peebles himself.

Towards five o'clock in the afternoon, I went over once more to the barber's shop, and found it in the possession of little Peebles's two children. The boy, aged eight years, who could never be persuaded by his father to take a pair of shears in his hands for any useful purpose, was busily occupied in cutting his sister's hair, according to some highly fanciful pattern. He had persuaded the girl, who was a year younger than himself, to sit patiently. under a promise that she should cut his hair in return. When I inquired after little Peebles's deputy, the children told me he had just stepped out, neither of them knew exactly where, but the boy rather thought to an adjoining public-house, from which he offered to fetch him.

He was fetched, of course. It was full ten minutes before he came; and when he entered the shop, his face looked very flushed, his eyes very sleepy, and he smelt very strongly of tobacco.

At this moment a strange gentleman came in, and took a seat.

" Shave ? " asked the deputy, thickly, addressing me.

" I'm in no hurry," I said, not altogether unselfishly, reserving the reproof I was about to administer to him for his neglect in leaving the premises.

" Right," he replied, slapping an open razor wildly, as he supposed upon his hand, but really upon the cuff of his greasy coat. " I can polish orf forty gents while old Peeblesh ish a-lookin' at one."

I was afraid, from his manner, that he was intoxicated; and while I affected to be deeply engaged with a newspaper, I watched him attentively.

H 2

" Any party can shave," he shouted, as he mixed a lather in
a way that shook the whole shop; "any party can shave—
man; but let 'em cut's 'air."

" I'm not in a hurry," said the stranger, mildly, after wincing
under the deputy's very vigorous application of the soap-brush.

" P'raps not, shir," said the deputy, slowly, as if giving
utterance to a very smart remark; " but y'see I am."

The stranger opened his eyes very widely upon hearing this
speech, and I moved about rather uneasily on my chair.

" Call shop a 'air-dresser's ? " continued the deputy, con-
temptuously, half-closing his right eye, wrinkling up his nose,
and partly putting out his tongue, while he covered the
stranger's face with lather; " no washes—no shampoo mix'ure
—no bucket de mill-flour—no nothink—bah ! "

As he delivered the latter part of this speech, he backed
towards a can of hot water, which was standing on a chair,
keeping his sleepy eyes fixed upon me, for the purpose, I suppose, of impressing me with what he was saying. Dipping
the open razor several times, without looking, down the outside of this can, under the impression that he had given it the
benefit of the water, he was returning unsteadily to complete
the shaving of the unsuspecting stranger, when I could remain
passive no longer.

" You're drunk," I said, starting up, "and I insist upon
your leaving this place immediately."

He was preparing a reply, when he was interrupted by the
entrance of a middle-aged gentleman, who brought in a child
—a little boy—whose head was cropped as closely and un-
evenly as if it had been under the hands of a prison barber.

" Where is Mr. Peebles ? " asked the middle-aged gentleman, hastily.

" He's not within at present," I replied, taking upon myself
the office of spokesman, while the stranger was hastily rubbing
the lather off his face with the jack-towel.

" I beg yer pardon," said the drunken deputy, pushing himself forward, " I beg yer pardon; Peeblesh is not in, but *I* am."

" I sent my child over here," continued the middle-aged gentleman, rapidly working himself into a passion, " to have his hair cut. Look at it! I don't know Mr. Peebles—I don't know the neighbourhood—I've only moved into it within the last twelve hours; and this is the treatment I receive through my only child."

" Shir," said the deputy, with an air of offended dignity, " you shent your boy over to common barbersh, an' you don't understan' a hartist's treatment."

The discussion, which now threatened to assume a serious aspect, was broken up in its beginning by the drunken deputy staggering out of the shop, and up the road towards London. I endeavoured to pacify the middle-aged gentleman, with some success, and I was aided materially by several of my neighbours, who came in, according to promise, to show their confidence in our barber's deputy.

We tried to keep this mishap, and several others which came to our knowledge, from little Peebles, but, of course, we failed. He thanked us all round for his holiday, but never showed any desire to take another. He still hangs up excursion bills of various kinds; and sometimes he talks vaguely of retiring at a distant period. I am afraid there is little prospect of such an occurrence. It is the fate of most men to die in harness, as it is called. That fate, I feel certain, will also be my barber's.

THE PHANTOM GENIUS.

PART I.

TOM MOLESKIN was a very excellent speci-
men of a common, uneducated working-man.
His ideas were very limited; his language
was even more limited; and his only ambition
was to work regularly, eat regularly, sleep regularly, culti-
vate pigeons on the top of his little house, and live near
where his bread grew—within sight of his factory chimney,

and within hearing of his factory bell. His little house, or castle, was in a back lane of Lambeth, not far from the river. It was not a very sightly building; for Tom's means were very humble, and he had to select a dwelling at a very moderate rent. Such houses as Tom required, lying close to the factory where he worked, were not very numerous, and the one he had now secured, old and ricketty as it was, was considered a prize by his fellow-workmen. Tom had even paid a small premium to buy out the last tenant, an idle, drunken workman, named Pothooks; and without having made any arrangement with the landlord for a lease, he considered that he had cast his domestic anchor for the next ten or twenty years.

As soon as Tom's Dutch clock struck one every working-day morning, the factory bell was heard ringing, and in a few minutes Tom always appeared, hungry and ready for his dinner. Mrs. Moleskin, his wife, was a steady, industrious working-woman, and always prepared for his appearance—sometimes with a little surprise in the shape of some extra delicacy, for Tom liked to live well. Any morning between twelve and one, she might have been seen in her blue check gown, large apron, and cap, bustling about the thinly-furnished room, which was both kitchen and parlour, arranging the plates and knives and forks on the table. She was so discovered on the morning when our little story opens.

" There goes the bell at the works," she said, as she lifted off the cover of a saucepan on the fire. " I'm rather behind-hand to-day, because of those people calling. Tom 'll be home in a minute, and he always likes his dinner ready when he comes in." She had hardly uttered these words before Tom made his appearance. He was a man about forty, dressed in thick, dark corduroy trousers, which were half-covered with brickdust; a red plush waistcoat, with pearl buttons; a dark-blue check shirt, a flannel jacket with pockets, a cap, and a red necktie. His shoes were muddy, his face was dirty at the lower part with a stiff beard, and his hair was rather grey.

"Now, Nancy," he said, hanging up his cap behind the door, "dinner ready?"

"Yes, Tom," returned Mrs. Moleskin.

"What is it?" asked Tom, advancing to the table.

"Well, dear," said Mrs. Moleskin, "I've killed one of the fowls."

"Which one?"

"Old Betsy."

"Old Betsy!" exclaimed Tom; "what, the old hen as was always moping about? I say——"

"Now, don't be stupid," said Mrs. Moleskin, taking off the cover; "you'll see what a nice dinner it'll make; its boiled."

"With inguns?" asked Tom.

"Yes," returned Mrs. Moleskin, helping her husband very liberally, and seating herself opposite him.

"Good!" said Tom, with his mouth full, eating voraciously; "heavy day at the works to-day."

"Oh!" replied Mrs. Moleskin, rather absently.

"Head overseer out o' sorts, too," continued Tom.

"I've got a good deal to tell you, Tom," said Mrs. Moleskin, without seeming to notice what her husband was saying.

"What's the matter?" asked Tom, with his mouth full.

"I've had visitors," returned Mrs. Moleskin, mysteriously.

"Don't talk with your mouth full," said Tom, reprovingly. "Who was it? Old Mother Brisket?"

"No; a lady and gentleman."

"No Board o' Works humbug, I hope?"

"No, Tom," returned Mrs. Moleskin, quickly and indistinctly, almost choking herself; "it was a young lady and gentleman; and they walked about, and they talked, and they looked round the room, and they read something from a newspaper, and they said it was the birthplace of Hooks or Crooks, or something o' that sort; and they said that when the young lady's father read it at his club, he would come down at once in a cab; and they asked when you would be in, and——"

"Halloo, Nancy!" said Tom, astonished. "what are you talking about? Young lady and gentleman—newspaper—old gent—club—come down in a cab—birthplace of Hooks or Crooks! What's the birthplace of Hooks or Crooks?"

"This house, Tom; they said he was born in that room," returned Mrs. Moleskin, pointing to the door of a small apartment, which served them as a bedroom.

"Who was born in that room?" asked Tom, in a bewildered manner. "Our Billy?"

"No, no," returned Mrs. Moleskin, "Hooks or Crooks."

"Who's Hooks or Crooks?" inquired Tom, getting out of temper.

"Oh, some great poet writer or other," returned Mrs. Moleskin. "I don't know."

At this point of the dinner-table conversation, a tapping was heard at the street-door, which had no knocker, and opened with a latch.

"Come in," said Tom, loudly, with his mouth half-full of potato, turning partly round upon his chair.

The invitation was at once accepted by the persons outside, and a lady and gentleman, dressed rather extravagantly, and both carrying eye-glasses, entered the room. The lady was thin and middle-aged, with a rather red nose, and grey hair arranged in curls on each side of her face. They walked in with a patronizing air, and a look of abstraction and inquisitiveness; and while the lady looked eagerly round the place through her eye-glass, the gentleman referred to a newspaper which he carried in his hand. Mrs. Moleskin regarded these visitors with curiosity; but Tom glared at them rather sullenly, with a knife in one hand, and a large piece of bread in the other.

"Is this the party?" Tom asked his wife, as the visitors were looking round the room.

"No," replied Mrs. Moleskin, "this is some one else."

"Now, sir," said Tom, rising and facing his visitors, and addressing the gentleman, "what can I do for *you?*"

"Don't disturb yourself, my good man, I beg," replied the gentleman, looking about the room. "We have merely come to pay our tribute to the shrine of genius. You may not be aware of it, but you are now standing in the birthplace of the immortal Pothooks. Go on with your dinner."

"Finish your dinner, my good man," continued the lady, abstractedly, also looking about the room; "and let us feed on those sweet memories which hover over the hearth that was once honoured by the presence of the immortal Pothooks."

"Thank'ee, mum," returned Tom, sulkily, eating his bread.

"Very neatly put, Penelope," said the gentleman, addressing the lady, almost without noticing Tom and his wife; "I'll make a note of that."

"Perhaps at this table, Alonzo," returned the lady, advancing to a small table at the side of the room, and addressing the gentleman, "in this very room, were composed those noble, heart-stirring poems, 'The Doctor's Boy,' and the 'Ode to Apoplexy!'"

"Very neatly put, Penelope," answered the gentleman, "very neatly put; and very likely it was on this chair he sat." As he spoke, he seated himself on a chair, the seat of which gave way, and nearly let him down.

"Take care, sir," said Mrs. Moleskin, interposing, "that's shaky."

"He couldn't have sat on that, either," said the gentleman, struggling up on his feet, "for he was a very heavy man."

Tom Moleskin regarded his strange visitors all this while with cool astonishment, following them with his eyes, and evidently trying to understand the meaning of their language and their visit. He soon came to a conclusion which was rather inhospitable.

" Now, I dare say," said Tom, " it may seem imperent to you what I'm about to observe ; but I want to know what the deuce you do walking about my room at dinner-time, as if it was the Natural Gallery or the British Mooseum ? "

" Sir ? " said the gentleman, in astonishment.

" Sir to you ! " returned Tom, getting excited. " Take off your hat in a gen'leman's house ! "

The eccentric male visitor did as he was requested, and the lady took up the conversation.

" We have come," she said, " to perform a sacred duty we owe to the memory of Pothooks—the divine Pothooks."

" I don't know anything about the divine Pothooks, mum," said Tom, " and I don't care. This apartment's mine, and the rent's paid. Nancy, purduce the rent-book."

" Here it is, Tom," returned Mrs. Moleskin, handing him a small red account-book taken from a drawer of the dinner-table.

" What grovelling ignorance ! " exclaimed the lady, addressing no one in particular.

" I beg pardon," interposed the gentleman, " but I think you are under a mistake. Pothooks — the divine Pothooks, the great poet—we have every reason to believe, was born here. For years an anxious and admiring body of literary gentlemen have been endeavouring to ascertain the exact house with something like precision ; and only this morning the learned and indefatigable editor of the *Weekly Mooner* was able to say, ' This is the house—No. 9, Stoker's-lane, Lambeth.' You will find it so stated in this newspaper."

" What right's he to put my house in a paper ? " asked Tom, indignantly. " If I don't bring an action for labelling, my name's not Tom Moleskin."

" Is it possible," asked the lady, " that you can hear without emotion that you stand in the very room which Pothooks has immortalized?"

"Read him that noble passage in the book you have in your pocket, Penelope," said the gentleman, "'Ode to Apoplexy,' page 40."

"Now, look here," replied Tom, trying to exert great command over himself, "I'm a working man; I go to my work every morning at six; I knock off at one to get my dinner, and I've just got a hour to eat it in. You see that clock, and you see that dinner. One stands at half-arter one, and t'other's getting cold. If Pothooks was born here, it's a pity he didn't leave the place in better repair, that's all I can say. There's the door: Nancy, show 'em out."

"Yes, Tom," replied Mrs. Moleskin, going to the door.

"Brief occupant of an immortal tenement," said the gentleman, "I scorn to commit violence in a place rendered sacred by the memory of Pothooks; otherwise——"

"I'm not going to put myself in a passion with you," said Tom, advancing; "but if you don't go out of that immortal door, I shall pitch you out of that immortal window."

Tom began to take off his jacket, but Mrs. Moleskin interfered, and the lady and gentleman went towards the door.

"Come, Penelope, come!" said the gentleman; "that ever fate should have thrown the birthplace of the immortal Pothooks into the hands of such a rude boor!"

Tom, by this time, had returned to the dinner-table; but, upon hearing this last expression, he again began to take off his jacket, and Mrs. Moleskin again interposed to preserve peace.

"Farewell, dear spot," said the lady, with a romantic sigh, "at once found and lost!"

"I've written my name in every corner of the place," whispered the gentleman to his companion, as they went out. Mrs. Moleskin immediately bolted the door after them.

"Pothooks! confound Pothooks!" exclaimed Tom, indignantly, walking about the room; "why, that's the old fool we took this house of, who comes in here drunk nearly every day to borrow money for gin!"

"Yes, Tom," replied Mrs. Moleskin, "and that's the name the young lady and gentleman mentioned this morning."

"Oh, it is, is it?" said Tom; "then we shall have another lot here."

"They said the young lady's father would be sure to be here in a cab, as I told you."

"Blest if I don't make a show of it," said Tom, sarcastically, "and charge a shilling each."

This idea seemed to pacify Tom a little, and he sat down to finish his dinner, which was now nearly cold. Before he could begin, however, another tapping was heard at the door.

"Who's there?" shouted Tom, furiously, jumping up from his chair.

"It's me, Tom—young Johnson," said a voice outside.

"What, Master Edmund?" exclaimed Tom, in a very altered tone, as he opened the door, "how are you?"

"How d'ye do, Tom?" said a good-looking, cheerful young man, shaking Tom by the hand, and entering the room, followed by a genteel young lady.

"Allow me to introduce Miss Maresnest—Mrs. Johnson that is to be," continued the new visitor, gaily pushing the young lady forward, and skipping lightly about the apartment.

"Nonsense, Edmund!" said the young lady, blushing; "how you do go on!"

"This is the young lady and gentleman," said Mrs. Moleskin, crossing over to her husband, "who called this morning."

"No!" replied Tom; "and didn't you know Master Edmund, that you have heard me talk of—the son of our head foreman at the yard?"

"I never saw him, you know, dear," said Mrs. Moleskin, as she walked on one side with Miss Maresnest.

"Well, now, Tom, to business," exclaimed young Johnson, stopping his dance about the room, and speaking to Tom Moleskin. "This is a serious job about this house."

"What house?" returned Tom, in his old sullen manner.

"This house—your house; the birthplace of Pothooks."

"Hang Pothooks! You're not going to worry me, are you?"

"There's no mistake about it," said young Johnson; "you'll have to leave."

"What for?" asked Tom, in a loud voice and a bewildered manner. "Is this my castle, or is it not? I'm a working man——"

"Now, Tom," replied young Johnson, "don't excite yourself, and be practical. Old Maresnest, the father of that young lady there, will have this house over your head, if he gives twenty thousand pounds for it. It is the dream of his life to possess the birthplace of the immortal Pothooks."

"Why didn't he come forward, then, and bid like a man?" inquired Tom, still in a very loud voice.

"But," interposed young Johnson.

"Oh, I hate anything underhand," continued Tom, interrupting him in an indignant tone.

"But," continued young Johnson, "he couldn't tell till to-day that Pothooks, the poet, was born here."

"There's been no Pothooks, the poet, ever born here," said Tom, with a strange expression on his face, intended to represent contempt at everybody's ignorance and stupidity. "Old dirty Pothooks, as I took the place of, used to live here, and a nice state he left it in!"

"Perhaps so, Tom," returned young Johnson, "perhaps so; and that may be the Pothooks that old Maresnest and all these people are after by mistake; but, for all that, you'll have to leave this house."

"I think it's precious hard," replied Tom, sulkily, "that just as I've settled down in a place within sight of the works, where I can hear the bell sound, after waiting patiently for two years, and buying one old Pothooks out, I'm to be bundled out myself, because a lot of fools fancy another old Pothooks was born here! I put it to you as a man: I put it to any man——".

"Troublesome, Tom, I admit; but you'd better submit like a sensible fellow. An enthusiast like old Maresnest is not to be opposed by any rational means."

"Look here, Nancy," shouted Tom, turning to his wife, "here's a pretty go! We must look out for another lodging."

"Yes, Tom," returned Mrs. Moleskin, advancing with Miss Maresnest; "the young lady has told me all about it."

"I'm a working man," said Tom, rather sulkily, to Miss Maresnest; "I go to work at six in the morning. I knock off at one——"

"Yes, yes," said young Johnson, interrupting him, "we know all that, Tom. Now, I want you to do me a service."

"Well, Master Edmund," returned Tom, a little less sulkily, "what is it?"

"I need not tell you," said young Johnson, smiling, "that this young lady and I are rather—rather fond of each other."

Mrs. Moleskin laughed at this speech, and Miss Maresnest blushed and simpered. Tom Moleskin made a jocular remark to his wife as he nudged her in the side, and told young Johnson to "go on."

"But what I need tell you," continued young Johnson, in answer to this request, "is, that her father, who happens to be her guardian, is mad upon the subject of the immortal Pothooks, and will never consent to her marrying any one but a descendant of that phantom celebrity."

"Good gracious!" ejaculated Tom.

"This obstacle to our union can only be removed by one

brilliant stroke of policy—a very pardonable piece of deception, under the circumstances. You must become the son-in-
law of the immortal Pothooks, Mrs. Moleskin his daughter,
and I the grandson on the mother's side."

"What! son-in-law of old, dirty Pothooks?" exclaimed Tom,
restlessly. "Come!"

"No, no," said young Johnson, pettishly, "the immortal
Pothooks, you know."

"No, I don't know; I can't go through all that!"

"Oh, I'm sure you can," interposed Miss Maresnest, per-
suasively. "Pa 'll never find it out—he'll only be too glad to
find so many descendants of Pothooks for that; and we shall
help to cure him of a very ridiculous and expensive mania."

At this juncture a knocking was heard at the street-door.

"I'll stand by you, and do all the speaking," said young
Johnson, hurriedly; "you leave it to me."

"The knocking was repeated.

"Perhaps that is pa?" suggested Miss Maresnest; and the
remark caused young Johnson and Mrs. Moleskin to disappear
in the side room. Tom got very fidgetty, and looked restlessly
at the clock, and gulped in his breath. Miss Maresnest walked
to the window.

"Well," said Tom, desperately, "I'm in for it now, so here
goes. Come in!" he shouted at the top of his voice.

This invitation was responded to by a young, shabby-looking
man, who passed through the door rapidly, turned round
quickly, and closed it, fastening the bolt, and then looked
inquiringly at Tom Moleskin.

"Halloo there!" shouted Tom, looking with astonishment
on this curious proceeding, "what are you bolting my door
for?"

"Ah! I beg pardon," said the new visitor, advancing, and
speaking confidentially to Tom; "are you the proprietor?"

"Yes," replied Tom, sulkily, "I suppose I am."

"Has any one been here—any photographic artist—to take a picture of this place?"

"Not as I'm aware on."

"Good," returned the new visitor. "Is she"—he added, pointing to Miss Maresnest—"anything in that way?"

"No," replid Tom.

"Good again," said the new visitor. "Now, look here," he continued, handing a card to Tom, "I'm a first-class photographic artist—there's my card. I don't like to touch anything that's not exclusive; you understand?"

"Can't say I do," replied Tom, becoming more sulky, and more bewildered.

"If you want a pound, you can have it," returned the first-class photographic artist, drawing nearer to Tom, and whispering in his ear; "but I must get a week's start with the picture of Pothooks's birthplace. You comprehend now?"

"Can't say I do," replied Tom.

"Oh, these working-classes!" exclaimed the first-class photographic artist, though not loud enough for Tom to hear what he said. "I must take a picture of this place," he added, addressing Tom, "and no other artist must be admitted for a week. Quick!" he continued, excitedly, "is that a bargain? I hear that confounded Stipple in the street."

A violent knocking was heard at the little street-door, which shook with the blows delivered on it from the outside.

"I don't know who you are," said Tom, sullenly, "and I don't know who you may be; but may I trouble you to open that door?"

"And admit Stipple?" inquired the first-class photographic artist, rather pettishly. "Very good," he added, "very good. If you're deaf to your own interest, I can't help it."

The knocking was still continued.

"Oh, yes!" said the first-class photographic artist, as he threw open the door, "of course; there!"

I

The door was no sooner thrown open, than in rushed another shabby-looking young man, very much like the first visitor. He was followed by a dirty boy, who struggled in with a photographic apparatus, a large box, a three-legged stand, and a curtain, all complete.

" Now, then !" shouted Tom, looking upon this apparition with increased wonder and disgust; "what game d'ye call this ?"

" Upon my word," said the second visitor, with the greatest confidence, almost disregarding Tom, "artists are nicely treated now-a-days : any one would think the birth-place of genius was not public property !"

" These fellows seem to make themselves wonderfully at home," said Tom, looking almost bewildered, first at one visitor, then at the other.

" I suppose I'm indebted to you, Mr. Burin," said the second visitor, addressing the first visitor, "for this temporary lock-out ? I owe you one, dear sir; I owe you one."

The first visitor—the first-class photographic artist, as he called himself—seemed to despise this remark, and instead of making any reply, he went to the window near where Miss Maresnest was standing, opened it, and looked out.

" Bill,'' he said to some one in the street, "come in ;" and another dirty boy struggled in with another photographic apparatus, very similar to the first. Both the boys proceeded to pitch their instruments in what they considered the best situations for their masters, and in doing this they first came to words, and then to blows.

" Come out of that !" shouted Tom, rushing forward, and pushing them out of the door; "if anybody wants to fight, I can tackle 'em."

" Proprietor, sir ?" asked the second visitor, addressing Tom.

" No," said Tom, with an attempt at sarcasm, " no proprietor at all ! Liberty Hall !"

" That's my card," returned the second photographic artist,

giving Tom a small card. The two rival artists then made preparations at the back to take views of the place, as coolly as if they had bought the lease, furniture, and fixtures, or were brokers' men sent in to make an inventory. They got very much in each other's way, and seemed inclined to break out into an open quarrel at any moment.

"There comes papa," said Miss Maresnest, excitedly, tripping down from the window, and addressing Tom; "full speed, as I expected, in a cab."

Mrs. Moleskin and young Johnson, hearing this, came out of the side room to have another hurried conference, and to arrange for the reception of old Mr. Maresnest.

"Now, then, for the little plot," said young Johnson, rubbing his hands; "it's sure to work well."

"I don't much like this business," said Tom, nervously, addressing his wife.

"Oh, I don't mind, if you don't," replied Mrs. Moleskin, who seemed more confident.

"What am I?" asked Tom, bewildered, speaking to young Johnson; "I'm sure to muddle it."

"The son-in-law of the immortal Pothooks," answered young Johnson; "I am the grandson on the mother's side, and Mrs. Moleskin is to personate the daughter. Emma—Miss Maresnest—will appear as if she had just arrived to inspect the premises."

"Very—well," responded Tom, very slowly.

The little group hastily arranged themselves round the dinner-table, with the exception of Miss Maresnest; and the two artists, who seemed to have either finished their views of the sitting-room, or to be anxious to seize upon some other points in the side room, both rushed into the last apartment, with sketching-books, and closed the door. The noise of wheels was heard outside, and, in a few moments, old Mr. Maresnest burst into Tom Moleskin's room.

PART II.

Mr. Maresnest was an elderly gentleman, tall, and not very stout; he wore spectacles, through which his eyes glittered eagerly; his dress was old-fashioned; and his necktie was an enormous white bandage. He looked a kind of man to attract furniture dealers, jobbers in old books and works of art. His manner was restless, hasty, and excited, but it was easy to see that he was very impressionable. He liked to possess rarities, or what were supposed to be rarities; and he liked to make discoveries, or what were supposed to be discoveries. Like all "collectors," as they are called, from collectors of pictures to collectors of poor-rates, he was eminently selfish.

"Bless my heart!" he said, speaking hurriedly, as he plunged into Tom Moleskin's humble sitting-room, "what an astonishing thing, to be sure! I must have been past this house a hundred times, without having the slightest idea that it was Pothooks's birthplace. I thought it was in quite a different direction. It was that precious snuff-shop at Islington which threw me off the scent; I traced the immortal Pothooks there, and then I lost him."

"Papa," said Miss Maresnest, advancing, "you see I've got the start of you."

"Halloo, minx!" returned Mr. Maresnest, not at all astonished to see his daughter, whom he left pretty much to take care of herself, while he indulged his hobby of curiosity-hunting. "What, are you here? How did you find it out?"

"In the same way as you did, papa; in the *Weekly Mooner*."

"Ha!" continued Mr. Maresnest, enthusiastically, "little did I imagine what a surprise awaited me when I reached the club. Little Button came up to me, and said, 'Have you heard the news?' 'No,' said I; 'what news?' 'Well,' said he, 'they've found out Pothooks's birthplace at last!' 'No!' said I—and you might have knocked me down with a penny pamphlet—' where ? ' ' In Lambeth,' said he; ' found it out by an old washerwoman's bill; you'll see it all in the *Weekly Mooner*.' I flew to that learned and enterprising print, and found it all true; and I hastened on here at once."

" Ah! papa," replied Miss Maresnest, " I think I've made a greater discovery than the editor of the *Weekly Mooner*."

" Speak, child," exclaimed Mr. Maresnest. " What is it ? "

" Well," replied Miss Maresnest, " I believe I've discovered that the persons in possession of the house claim to be descendants of the illustrious Pothooks."

" Gracious goodness!" shouted Mr. Maresnest, " where are they ? Are they here ?"

By this time young Johnson had arranged Mrs. Moleskin and Tom at the little dinner-table, in what he considered a proper romantic, attitudinising group. Mrs. Moleskin was passive, but Tom was rather sulky, and difficult to deal with.

" Let me introduce to you, papa," said Miss Maresnest, pointing to this group, " the persons who claim to be the daughter, the son-in-law, and the grandson on the mother's side, of the poet Pothooks."

" Is it possible," exclaimed Mr. Maresnest, regarding them with enthusiastic astonishment, " that I look upon the intimate connexions of that immortal man of genius, whose traces I thought at one time I had lost for ever ?"

At this moment the work-bell of the neighbouring factory, where Tom Moleskin was employed, rang loudly, to summon the labourers back from dinner.

" I must be off," shouted Tom, starting up, and nearly knocking young Johnson down in his haste, " or I shall get the sack!"

" Never, sir!" said Mr. Maresnest, very excited, and restraining Tom; " never, sir, not for all the factory bells in England !"

" Sir ? " said Tom, evidently misapprehending Mr. Maresnest's meaning.

"I say, not for all the factory bells in England!" continued Mr. Maresnest, raising his voice. "Shall I, after years of patient labour and watchfulness, which have led me to—to—to the only living link that binds me to the past—the past of the immortal Pothooks—allow that link to—to—to go from my gaze to a menial and dirty employment?"

"What do you mean, sir?" asked Tom, excitedly; "I'm a working-man!"

"For goodness' sake, calm yourself," said young Johnson, speaking quietly to Tom, "or we shall spoil all. My supposed uncle, sir," he added, addressing himself to Mr. Maresnest, "the reputed son-in-law of the immortal Pothooks, did not quite apprehend your meaning. Long years of obscurity and neglect have made him rather touchy."

Mr. Maresnest walked rapidly round the room, looking at the furniture, after this speech, followed by young Johnson. Mrs. Moleskin and Miss Maresnest stood together on one side, and Tom took a pipe from his pocket and filled it with tobacco.

"Light, Nancy," said Tom to his wife; and when Mrs. Moleskin brought it to him, he lighted his pipe and smoked rather sulkily.

"A pretty game's been going on all this blessed dinner-time," he remarked, in a grumbling tone. "People walking about the room as if it was the Crystal Palace; people wanting to read poetry at me; people wanting to take pictures; and now I'm to lose half a day's work, and perhaps get the sack. I put it to you, sir," he called out to Mr. Maresnest, "I put it to any man! I'm a working-man; I go to work at six in the morning——"

"I can quite understand your feelings," replied Mr. Maresnest, advancing to Tom; "but be under no concern. Is this apartment in the same state as when he left it?" he added, glancing eagerly round the room.

"Who left it?" asked Tom, sullenly.

"The immortal Pothooks, of course. Do be careful," said young Johnson, prompting Tom Moleskin.

"Pothooks—the immortal Pothooks?" continued Mr. Maresnest.

"No," said Tom, "it was precious dirty when he left it."

Young Johnson gave Tom a nudge.

"Sir?" said Mr. Maresnest.

"I've had it whitewashed," returned Tom, loudly, "and put on another paper."

"Oh, but you should'nt have done that!" replied Mr. Maresnest, excitedly.

Young Johnson fidgeted about the room.

"How d'ye mean?" asked Tom, still sucking his pipe.

"Why—why," answered Mr. Maresnest, hastily, "there may have been some very valuable writing on the wall!"

"Oh, no," continued Tom, chuckling in a peculiar and confident manner, "he couldn't write."

"What!" exclaimed Mr. Maresnest, in astonishment.

"Do think of the immortal Pothooks, not the last tenant!" whispered young Johnson, addressing Tom, excitedly. "Pothooks—the immortal Pothooks, we're speaking of."

"But I took the place of old dirty Pothooks," answered Tom, whispering to young Johnson in his turn.

"Yes, yes!" continued young Johnson, impatiently. "It is very true, sir," he added, addressing Mr. Maresnest, that during the latter years of the supposed immortal Pothooks's life he could *not* write; of course, I speak of penmanship, and not of composition; his fertile mind was as full of vigour and fancy as ever, but the feeble hand refused to obey its dictates, and he had to employ a copying-clerk when the inspiration was on him."

"Good gracious!" returned Mr. Maresnest, "what an interesting literary fact! When did this weakness come upon him?—as near as you can guess, now?"

"Well," said young Johnson, appear
"we should say about—about 1810."

"Or twenty," added Tom.

"Ah!" replied Mr. Maresnest, chuckl
"that destroys all the autographs afte
Button's letters that he prized so, then, a

"No doubt of it, sir," remarked young

"Have you made any other alterations
nest, addressing Tom, and again glancing

"Yes," said Tom, "altered the chimley

"Why?"

"'Cos it smoked."

Young Johnson again nudged Tom.

"Dear, dear!" exclaimed Mr. Maresn
should'nt have done that. It's the most in
house. He wrote a poem on it!"

"Now, look here," said Tom, doggedl
man! I go to work at six in the morning

"Do be careful Tom," again whispe
'you're breaking out again."

"I don't care," said Tom, sulkily; "is tl
not?"

"I must preserve this sacred edifice from
remarked Mr. Maresnest, speaking to him
owe to society."

"My respected supposed uncle, here, si
Johnson, addressing Mr. Maresnest, "has i
honesty which distinguished his reputed i
—the great Pothooks. He means well, but
in expressing himself."

"I can understand and appreciate that character," said Mr.
Maresnest. "But," he added, addressing Tom, "you can give
me most interesting information about your immortal father-in-
law. What were his habits generally?"

"The old gent wants to hear about my father-in-law, now," said Tom to himself, "as well as old Pothooks. These people are not at all curious—oh no! My father-in-law?" he added, addressing Mr. Maresnest; "oh, he used to play a good deal at skittles."

"Bless my heart!" exclaimed Mr. Maresnest, astonished; "is it possible?"

"Ah! I believe you," continued Tom, warming up a little; "and if he couldn't bring 'em down, I don't know who could."

"No doubt that illustrious man excelled even at skittles, as he did at everything else. Go on; you interest me strangely. Was he regular in his ways?"

"He used to get drunk every Saturday night."

"Dear, dear!" exclaimed Mr. Maresnest; "the wanderings of a man of genius!"

"Yes," said Tom, "and we had no end o' trouble to get him to bed."

"Ah!" remarked Mr. Maresnest, "his mighty intellect, fired by drink, refused to submit to the ordinary trammels and restrictions of domestic prudence."

"Very likely, sir," said Tom; "he nearly set the house o' fire."

"This house?" exclaimed Mr. Maresnest, very much startled.

"Yes," answered Tom; "any house, it didn't matter to him."

"What an awful picture!" continued Mr. Maresnest, musingly. "Pothooks and his birth-place consumed in one funeral pyre!"

"Then he used to get the blue-devils of a morning," returned Tom, "and want to cut his throat—stupid old fool!"

"Dear, dear! what a heartrending picture! Did he seem to labour much at his works?"

"What works? the gas-works?"

"No, no; his writing—his composition?"

" Oh! bless you, no; he never went to work afore Wednesday."

" Was his appetite pretty good ?" continued Mr. Maresnest.

" I should think it was," answered Tom Moleskin, laughing.
" Here, Nancy," he added, addressing his wife, " how about
father's appetite ?   It was'nt particularly·delicate, was it ?"

" Not very, Tom," answered Mrs. Moleskin, laughing, and
advancing with Miss Maresnest and young Johnson.

" He used to punish a leg o' mutton, eh ?" asked Tom.

" Rather, Tom," answered Mrs. Moleskin, still laughing.
Young Johnson again nudged Tom, and warned him quietly to
be careful.

" I dare say you can answer me one question that will settle
a very curious point," continued Mr. Maresnest.   " Was your
illustrious father ever in Australia ?"

" Was he, Nancy ?" asked Tom, addressing his wife.

" No, never out of England," answered Mrs. Moleskin.

" Never out o' England at all," continued Tom.

" Very remarkable, indeed," exclaimed Mr. Maresnest;
" wonderful !"

" I know another man," said Tom, smoking his pipe, " who
was never out o' England."

" You know that passage in his poems which has been
debated so much ?   How does it go ?   My memory's not very
good."

" What game's up now ?" remarked Tom to himself.   " Can't
say I do," he added, aloud.

Young Johnson and Mrs. Moleskin walked back to the table.

" Do you mean in the ' Ode to Apoplexy,' papa ?" asked
Miss Maresnest, stepping forward.

" Blest if I don't think they're all rather cranky," again
remarked Tom to himself, as he looked on astonished.

" No," returned Mr. Maresnest, " in the minor poems.
Hum! I've got it on the tip of my tongue, too."

" Oh! I know, papa," answered Miss Maresnest, "it goes—

> "' But my heart is in the wild Australian woodlands,
> With the gum-tree and the bounding kangaroo.'"

" Exactly!" exclaimed Mr. Maresnest, delightedly, "that's
it! 'With the gum-tree and the bounding kangaroo.' What
a remarkable local colouring is thrown over that passage? It's
perfect! The 'gum-tree,' and we know that he was never in
Australia! And the 'bounding kangaroo,' too; how natural!
Observe the 'bounding,'" he continued, giving a most absurd
pantomimic imitation of what he considered to be the chief
moving characteristic of the animal described.

Tom followed these motions with unconcealed wonder de-
picted in his stolid face; Mrs. Moleskin fairly burst out laughing,
and young Johnson tried to stop her mouth with her apron.

" Why, the old gent's worse than the young'un," said Tom;
" he's as mad as a March hare!"

" True, sir," observed young Johnson, advancing to Mr.
Maresnest, and leaving Mrs. Moleskin at the table; " if my
supposed illustrious grandfather on the mother's side had
written nothing but that one simple poem, it would have
stamped him as a man of genius!"

" Nobly observed, young gentleman," returned Mr. Maresnest, approvingly. " I'm glad to find that you appreciate the
beauties of the great Pothooks. You show a taste and
discernment above your years."

" Well," said Tom to himself, with an inward chuckle,
" blest if ever I could see any beauty in Pothooks."

At this juncture, a muffled noise was heard in the side room,
where the two photographic artists had retired some little time
before.

" Halloo there!" shouted Tom, " what game d'ye call that?"
and he rushed to see what the noise was about, followed by
Mrs. Moleskin.

"I have deeply studied him, sir," continued young Johnson, addressing Mr. Maresnest, as though there had been no interruption, "not because he was a reputed relative, but because he was a true poet."

"Very nicely observed," remarked Mr. Maresnest. "Don't you think so?" he added, turning to Miss Maresnest.

"Oh! yes, papa," returned that young lady, impressively.

"I am glad, sir, to perceive," continued Mr. Maresnest, addressing young Johnson, "that you have become imbued with some portion of the spirit which hovers about these walls."

"If the mantle of the immortal Pothooks has not fallen upon me," answered young Johnson, "in all its solid reality, I am proud and happy to say that I have received at least its shadow."

After young Johnson had delivered this high-flown speech, in a melancholy tone, he walked to another part of the room.

"A relative," said Mr. Maresnest to himself, looking at young Johnson; "youthful, with some share of the genius of the immortal Pothooks! Why should I hesitate! I might become the grandfather of a Pothooks! It is a duty that I owe to society. Emma!" he added, speaking to Miss Maresnest.

"Yes, papa," readily answered that young lady.

"You've always been a sensible girl—thanks to my teaching—with a sympathy for genius, in whatever form it presents itself."

"Now it's coming," said Miss Maresnest to herself. "Yes, papa," she added, aloud.

"Could you, from a high sense of literary duty," asked Mr. Maresnest, "devote yourself to that worthy grandson of the immortal Pothooks—become his wife?"

"Well, papa," said Miss Maresnest, blushing, "from a sense of the duty I owe to society, I think I could."

"Noble, disinterested child!" exclaimed Mr. Maresnest. "Ah—young man," he added, calling to young Johnson, who came forward, "take my daughter, and confer upon her the distinction of being united to a descendant of the immortal Pothooks."

"Thanks, generous benefactor!" replied young Johnson.

At this interesting moment a smashing of glass was heard, and the two photographic artists rolled out of the side room into the sitting-room, followed by Tom and Mrs. Moleskin.

"What the deuce d'ye mean by fighting in my rooms, disturbing the pigeons, and smashing the glass in that way?" shouted Tom, in a rage. "Is this my house, or is it not?"

The quarrel still continued between the rival artists, and Tom seized one of the photographic machines.

"Come out o' that," he shouted, addressing the two men, "or I'll knock you down with this machine. Who's going to pay me for my fourteen squares o' glass?"

The men took no notice of Tom, but still continued their quarrel; so he stripped off his jacket, and hustled them both out of the door.

"I've stood this quite long enough," said Tom, "so here goes;" and as he said this, he threw one of the photographic machines through the window into the street.

"Halloo!" said a rather thick, hoarse voice outside, "what are you up to? Pitching the bedstead out o' window?"

"Halloo!" said Tom, looking out. "Why, blest if there ain't old Pothooks," he added, turning to Mr. Maresnest, "and I've half smashed him!"

"Pothooks?" exclaimed the old gentleman.

"Yes, Pothooks," answered Tom; "he comes here nearly every day, and generally drunk."

While they were speaking, a rough-looking, middle-aged man, with filmy eyes and a red nose, entered the room. His boots were very muddy, his clothes rather ragged, and his face very dirty. His necktie was very loose, and he carried a short pipe in his hands. He was half tipsy.

"Thomas Moleskin," observed this new visitor, slowly, taking off an old smashed hat, and looking at it leisurely, " is this using an old friend well?"

"How did I know you was under the window?" returned Tom.

"Who is this person," said Mr. Maresnest, addressing Tom, "who bears the remarkable name of Pothooks?"

"Who? why, Pothooks himself, of course!"

"This can't be the immortal Pothooks?"

"Whoever said he was?" answered Tom. "You're not the immortal Pothooks," he added, addressing the dirty visitor, "are you, Jack?"

"Immor'al Pothooks?" said the dirty visitor, slowly, "oh, no!"

"You never wrote no poetry stuff," asked Tom, "nor anything o' that sort, did you, Jack?"

"Bless you, Tom," replied the dirty visitor, slowly, and in a pathetic tone, "I wouldn't do anything o' the sort for the world!"

"No!" said Tom.

"No!" said the dirty visitor.

"Well," said Mr. Maresnest, "but there must be some gross imposition here!"

"Now, look here!" said Tom; "I've heard a good deal about a man called the immortal Pothooks. I don't know him, and never said I did. This is *my* Pothooks—the mortal Pothooks. P'raps he was born here, p'raps he wasn't. That's about it, I think," he added, addressing the dirty visitor; "eh, Jack?"

"Quite right, Tom," said the dirty visitor; "my sen'iments exactly."

"Then we have still to search for the birthplace of the immortal Pothooks," said Mr. Maresnest, much crestfallen, "and I have given my daughter to——"

"A very good husband," said young Johnson, confidently

advancing, "although not bearing the remarkable name of Pothooks."

"No, thank goodness!" said Miss Maresnest, to herself.

"Now, look here!" said Tom Moleskin, "I'm a working-man——"

"Yes, yes," returned Mr. Maresnest, pettishly, "we know all that; but where's the birthplace of the immortal Pothooks?"

"How should I know?" said Tom Moleskin. "I put it to you as a man—I put it to any man—is this my house, or is it not? Whether Pothooks was born here or not, it doesn't much matter; for while I'm the party here, you look in at any time, and there's always a knife and fork for you."

EDMUND EVANS, Engraver and Printer, Raquet Court, Fleet Street.

CPSIA information can be obtained at www.ICGtesting.com
Printed in the USA
BVOW06s0126050915

416575BV00024B/911/P